the NAKED TRUTH ABOUT SEXUALITY

HAVILAH CUNNINGTON

FOREWORD BY BANNING LIEBSCHER

CHAPTER 5: SEX AND RESTORATION

CHAPTER 6: SEX AND COVENANT

ABOUT THE AUTHOR

I always knew God had a plan for other's lives, but never felt God could use me. I struggled with learning disabilities throughout my school years, which caused me to have great insecurity about my value and worth. It wasn't until the age of 17, as I was sitting in a car with friends on my way to a party, when I heard the voice of God speak to my heart, "There is more to life than this! I have called you. Come follow me." I spoke out in that moment, telling those in the car that I had a call on my life and they were welcome to come with me, but I was going to serve God.

I remember walking into our house when I got home, kneeling by my bed and saying these simple words, "God, I'm not much. I'm young, I'm a girl with no special gifting. But if You can use anyone, You can use me." Now, thinking back to that day, it makes me laugh at how I'd hoped the heavens would have opened up, with angels descending and ascending on a heavenly ladder. That didn't happen and I didn't need it to. God heard my cry and He was at work to accomplish His perfect will in my life.

By 19, my twin sister Deborah and I were traveling all over California preaching, teaching and singing at any place that would have us. By 21, we had been in seven different states and Mexico teaching about Jesus and His great plan for this generation!

I believe today is the Church's finest hour, if we choose to live with passion, purpose and walk in power. I'm passionate about seeing individuals encounter God in a real way and seek to blow the lid off common misconceptions, personal limitations and powerless living. My heart and passion is to inspire and challenge others to become all God has designed them to be.

— *Havilah Cunnington*

Havilah wears many hats: wife, mom, pastor, teacher, daughter and friend. She and her husband Ben were leaders at The Rock of Roseville Church for 15 years, before becoming the Directors of Moral Revolution. They enjoy spending time with their four young sons: Judah, Hudson, Grayson and Beckham. They currently reside in Redding, California.

FOREWORD

One of the main issues the Gospel addresses is the issue of powerlessness. God sent His Son, so that in every area of our lives we could experience His power. Years ago, I had a picture of Jesus walking into a room with a towel over his arm... etched with the word "serving". I felt Him say, "I am here tonight to serve those with addictions." In this picture, I saw people stand up across the auditorium holding a 3D word, "powerless." He came up to each person, took the word "powerless" and broke off the four letters at the end. He then gave them back the word "power."

Jesus died to release power into our lives and it is available to all who embrace it.

You and I are not created to live disconnected or powerless. We are meant to live connected and powerful. But for many of us, including those like myself who grew up in the church, we still feel alone and powerless in so many areas. Whether it's relationally, physically, emotionally, sexually, financially, or other areas... we sometimes live with a sense of detachment and powerlessness.

For the majority, I believe this is rooted in not understanding truth, where we haven't been given the tools or the skills to use those tools.

For example, I am extremely lost when it comes to anything to do with handyman work around the house. You know, odd jobs including plumbing... carpentry... electrical... things of that nature. Limited in my understanding, I have barely any tools, and was never taught the skills required to repair things. Therefore, I frequently find myself feeling inadequate and powerless in situations at my house. One particular time, my shower faucet wasn't working properly. I remember being paralyzed for days, not knowing what to do. I would stare at the faucet, but was clueless on where to start or how to fix the problem. Luckily, I have great friends who are more capable than I am! So I called my friend Jerry and asked him if he could come and help me. I showed him the faucet that had been taunting me for days. He examined it briefly, went to his car, opened his trunk, and pulled out a tool belt. "You have a tool belt in your car?" "Absolutely. I carry it everywhere I go." "Wow, if I have tools, I'm not sure where they are and I wouldn't even know how to use them." Jerry proceeded to fix my faucet in about three minutes. It was extremely easy — to him. I stood back, both surprised at how simple it was and slightly embarrassed I couldn't do it myself.

This is how so many of us feel in life — incomplete and powerless in areas God wants us to feel whole and powerful in. However, it takes understanding, tools — and the skills to use them — to step into a place of freedom and power.

For many of us, if not all, the issue of sexuality is one of the most confusing and powerless areas in our lives. We don't understand it, have no tools to deal with it, and lack the skills to navigate it in a healthy and Godly manner. While we are famous for shouting many things in the church, we merely whisper when it comes to the more difficult conversations around sexuality. No one really talks about it in the church or our families… and if they do it is brief, awkward and constricting. Therefore, the subject is often shunned and ignored.

Not outside the church though. The world is shouting about sexuality. Every billboard, TV show, magazine, book, and song we hear seems to be talking to us about sensuality and sexuality. Everywhere we turn it seems to be screaming, "SEX!"

The ironic fact is our God is not silent on this issue. And the Bible has a lot to say about sexuality.

I have seen the struggle firsthand. As a pastor, I have ministered for over two decades to youth and young adults, walked closely with adults, and even personally know the wrestling that comes with navigating sexuality. We all desire to find the wholeness and power our Father has purposed for us.

I love, LOVE, that Havilah has written a book on this subject. I can think of no one better suited to tackle this subject head-on. And tackle it head-on she has! While many in the church run from this topic or have allowed the culture to define for them what sexuality is all about, Havilah is a voice of freedom and hope. Using candid authenticity, she brings clarity to what God wants us to know. She turns the light of understanding on to what He intended. She reveals how God's design is not for you to live a life racked with guilt and anxiety… confused or tormented. She shouts the truth that you can be whole and powerful in your sexuality.

Havilah's insights into who you are, will release and empower you. This book is not just theory or theology, but practical and helpful. She unpacks the needs and desires you have — offering fundamentals you can be secure in. She encourages you to take care of the basics — understanding how your body, soul and spirit operate.

You do not have to believe the lies society is feeding you about sexuality. You do NOT have to live powerless. *The Naked Truth About Sexuality* will propel you toward experiencing freedom from shame and confusion.

You will not be the same after reading this book. I encourage you to grab a tool belt and get ready. God is going to fill you, break powerlessness off your life and overflow you with His completeness and ability. His Spirit replaces our faulty thinking and reveals to us His thoughts and ways.

My prayer is that you experience the freedom and power available to you, as well as bring life to others on your journey.

— *Banning Liebscher*

PREFACE

I was the 26-year-old virgin who bought every book on sex, love, relationships, and dating that the Christian world had to offer. I attended conferences, signed covenants, and went to alter calls looking for answers for the questions in my head. I read hungrily, listened attentively, and responded wholeheartedly. I needed to know: what was all of this about?

Faced with uncertainty and a multitude of new questions, I decided with the mass of the Evangelical church, to "kiss it all goodbye," and learned what it took to be a "courting girl" instead. I got my passion and purity on, habitually reading and rereading the same few scriptures (and they were few) about sex and marriage.

Later, after getting married, I found myself once again buying books on sex, love, marriage, and relationships. My husband and I went to pre-marital counseling, marriage retreats, and bi-annual marriage conferences. At times, we even sought professional counseling. We were getting tools to help us grow, but I still felt as if something was missing.

My head was filled with theological ideas and a desire to live right but I lacked confidence in my Biblical sexuality; and to be honest most of the church looks the same way. We know scriptures; we know the dos and don'ts. We may even make it to our wedding night with our virginity intact, by the skin of our chinny-chin-chin, but we lack something deep within.

When it comes to our sexuality, we do not need more strategies. We do not need more fear-based messages preached to motivate us into holiness. We do not need the mass of our churches hiding in shame, hoping no one discovers what happened before the wedding, or on our computers late at night.

What we need is more discovery of what is already inside of us. We need to learn about original design. We need to know that God made sex with a purpose and He designed us to be able to fully experience it. We need to know He made the whole of our sexuality and He is not confused, embarrassed, or ashamed of what He created. We need to know that He made our body to be deeply bonded to our spouse, connected emotionally and spiritually, and in ways and places no human eye can see. This is part of the beauty and mystery of sex.

Our questions need to be answered not with fear, shame, or uncertainty but with more love, power, and sound wisdom. As a church culture, we need to move away from "Don't, because it's bad for you," and move toward holistic answers that celebrate personal responsibility and levelheaded education. We all need to hear, "Here's how you were made and it is very good! Because of the way God made you, your decisions are powerful and will shape your life!" We need people to walk side-by-side with us as we find truth for questions like, "Why shouldn't we have sex outside of marriage?" Since God has given us access to so much more, we shouldn't have to give a "because it's wrong and I said so" kind of response. He has hidden the truth in plain sight.

But, then again, it's still a little hidden. We wonder, what's the right environment to learn or teach about sex? How do we get our sexual "needs" met when we're married? Look around! Society is not shy on this subject and has a lot to say about this. What I have come to realize is God isn't shy about it either. God has a lot to say on the subject, but it's hidden in our design just as much as in the scriptures.

Whether you are a young adult struggling to walk out purity, an engaged couple trying to answer the "why wait" question, a leader simply trying to help your student, or a parent desperately looking for tools to help your kids navigate puberty — I may know a little of where you're coming from. When I began to pastor almost two decades ago, I found many people asking the same questions I was trying to answer. Honestly, I became tired of men and women coming to me, looking for help, when all I could do was regurgitate answers I had heard or read. I lacked conviction. I lacked resolve. We were all in the same boat. So, I went to work, looking for answers.

I wanted to know about original design. I wanted to know about the "be fruitful and multiply" kind of sex. I wanted to know if what God said in the Bible was still relevant today. I wondered, is it still possible to teach purity in a society that glorifies sex?

Now, after years of research, conversations, studying scripture, and praying to know God's heart, I have resolve. I have a passion and a conviction that no one has to live powerlessly when it comes to their sexuality. I now know how God made me. I know how He made you. You see, what He established years ago is not out of date, out of style, or impossible to live. In fact, it's the most natural, realistic, and liberating way to live! Whether you are single, dating, engaged, married, or divorced, the tools and information in this book will be vital to the health of your relationships and how you steward your God given sexuality.

So, if you're sick of not knowing, eager to learn, or are just confused like I was, this book is for you! It will answer the questions you have. It will change the sexual legacy of your family. The Naked Truth About Sexuality is the beginning for you — for all of us — to start getting it right.

What are you waiting for? Let's begin!

—Havilah

01 | SEX And GOD

The Lord is slow to anger, abounding in love and forgiving sin and rebellion.
NUMBERS 14:18 (NIV)

① ON THE EVE OF THE FALL

Let's go back to the beginning, shall we? It's late in the day, cool in the shade. The sparrow lays her first egg, and a fawn soaks in the last bursts of sunlight. God is walking with Adam, He has just created Eve, and everything is, shall we say, good. "And the man and his wife were both naked and were not ashamed." Everything is going as God intended when, suddenly, the crafty serpent

> AND THE MAN AND HIS WIFE WERE BOTH NAKED AND WERE NOT ASHAMED

decides to have a field day in the garden. We all know what happens next. The happy couple is being escorted out of paradise with the voice of their Creator ringing in their ears:

" *Because of what you've done, Eve, pain will be a part of your life. From this day forward you'll give birth to your babies in pain. You'll want to please your husband, but he'll lord it over you. Adam, the very ground is cursed because of you; getting food from the ground will be as painful as having babies is for your wife; you'll be working in pain all your life long...* **"**

(GENESIS 3:16-19, MSG, WITH ADDITIONAL PARAPHRASE)

Wait — can we pause for a second here? Let's rewind and take it back. Things are good, the birds are chirping and things are all around pretty nice. God is walking in the garden with His two most precious creations — the ones He created in His image. Man and Woman. Guy and Girl. It seemed like things were going so well, weren't they? What happened between "it's good" and "get out"? Did God just reject those He made for His pleasure? Did something change? Did He change His mind?

To someone reading this story for the first time (alert: plot spoiler ahead), this might seem like an abrupt — and somewhat cruel — beginning to what is supposed to be the greatest love story written by the kindest God in the universe.

If you asked different people, I bet they would all give you different key words to describe this infamous event. Would it be disobedience? Separation? Pride? Unbelief?

Sin?

What happened exactly? I mean, we all know that the crafty serpent tricked Eve, and that Eve shared the fruit with Adam, disobeying God's instruction to keep away from the tree of the knowledge of good and evil.

The serpent said to the woman: "You will not certainly die, for God knows that when you eat from it your eyes will be opened, and you will be like God, knowing good and evil."

Was the problem that their eyes were opened? Was the problem that they suddenly knew good from evil? Or perhaps it was that they didn't believe what they had was good enough? Maybe they just didn't trust God's word?

Whatever it is you believe on the subject, the reality is that suddenly God's pure intention for creation became perverted, steering us away from what He desired for us. We've been trying to make our way back to the garden ever since.

So, let's go back to the Garden. Whether you know it or not, it seems we are all trying to get back there. It's the place where our identity dwells, and where our purpose is found. If we can realize that our beginnings were pure, beautiful and full of pleasure, we may find that our endings can also be — shall we say — happily ever after.

How about we start here: God created man and woman to fit together. He made them for His good pleasure, and for theirs. God made sex. Sex was God's idea. Therefore, sex is good.

Sex is also powerful. That's a no-brainer. Just look around at the way we are as a society — the way people communicate in media, in relationships, and in general language — and we can see that sex is a powerful tool used in both positive and negative ways. In English, many of our swear words are rooted in sex. Why? Sex is somehow taboo — provocative, suggestive, challenging — because we're offended by it, and yet completely obsessed with it. As much as we can focus on the negative aspects of the way it's used or abused, we must understand the reason why sex is powerful: because a man and a woman united together, as one, is the complete image of God. Both male and female He created them, in His image (Genesis 1:27). If we want to take back the power, we must take back the root. We must go back to the original design and have an honest conversation, open and unashamed, about what's going on.

> **IT'S TIME TO GET EDUCATED SO THAT WE CAN EDUCATE THE GENERATIONS TO COME**

We need to get real. It's time to get educated so that we can educate the generations to come. Let's get the facts, and embrace the God-given truth. There is nothing more important to the cause of freedom than the voice of truth because, simply, it's the truth that sets us free.

② THE MORNING AFTER

I grew up in church— literally. My father was a traveling evangelist, and I started preaching and leading worship in my teen years. I've been in ministry for nearly two decades. I've probably heard thousands of messages in my life and in all that time, I could count on one hand the number of times we talked about sex in church. In fact, we never really talked about sex. The only thing we ever talked about when it came to sex was that Adam knew Eve and that "knowing" is, well, you should just know what that means. Throughout the Bible there's this experience of "knowing" that occurs between two people. Take Genesis 38 for example:

❝*Then Judah identified them and said, "She is more righteous than I, since I did not give her to my son Shelah." And he did not know her again.***❞**

Or how about Matthew 1:25 when Joseph knew Mary not until she had given birth to a son? It depends on which translation you have, which may be a little more explicit for our wondering minds, but that's essentially what the church has done to us. We have just assumed that we should know about it (whatever it may be).

Being a church girl, I remember those sessions where we had what seemed like a purity "moment". Literally, a moment. You never heard about it before, and you never heard about it after. They would ask you to raise your hand, sign a covenant, or come up to the altar. Wanting to please God, and eagerly trying to fix all our cascading emotions and newly forming urges (which we'd later find out was a sex drive), we'd do it all. Then suddenly, it was all over. We were left alone at the altar, never really knowing what we signed up for, hoping we were "fixed" for now, or better yet, pure.

I remember when I made my own commitment to purity. One day, my dad excitedly announced he was going to be taking me on a date. I was to get all dressed up and he would take me to a surprise location for a surprise event. I enthusiastically signed up! He took me out on that date and gave me a ring — one that I still wear to this day — and asked me to sign a contract. The ring, the contract, the date, all represented his and my mom's desire to play a role in my life of purity. They wanted me to know that they loved me and I was not alone in this journey. I signed it saying, "Yes. I will commit!" but at 12 years old, I didn't really know what that meant. I liked the ring, and I wanted to wear it, but I really didn't know exactly what it was going to take. I didn't really know the significance of the commitment or the symbolism of the ring and signature. In the same way, much of the church doesn't understand the significance of their covenant with God, their commitment to purity, or the value of their choices. In fact, many are floundering, wondering what moral (or righteous and holy) behavior looks like.

As we look into scripture, we see various bits of the whole when it comes to sex. It seems to come down to three things: Don't look at your neighbor's wife because that's lust; don't look at somebody with lust because that's adultery, and absolutely do not have sex with your neighbor's wife because that's adultery, too. I don't know about you, but I think there's a lot that can happen between looking at someone's wife and going to bed with her. Needless to say, the church has been a little nervous, or can we just say silent, when talking about sex. What happened between Eden and today's church? What has happened to make us so uncomfortable talking about one of the most important subjects for us as human beings?

It seems that somewhere along the way, we got mixed messages. Some celebrate sex, some shame it, some idolize it, and some fear it. Some can't decide how they feel about it. Where did we learn to think this way? Is it the Puritans' fault? Do we blame pornography? Our parents?

③ THE ENVIRONMENTS

When my husband and I got married, we started having sex. As we began to build intimacy and know one another, we talked about our sexual histories and understandings, which turned out to vary greatly. How did two church-raised, God-fearing Christians end up with such different perspectives and understandings? Not to point fingers at our parents, but we came from very different environments when it came to sex. While my home was very open with everyone talking about it, in my husband's home they never talked about it. We began to realize that the environments we were raised in not only shaped our understanding and attitudes, but also our experience of sex. Our presumptions and preconceived notions shaped our ability (or lack thereof) to dialogue about sex in a healthy way.

> WHETHER YOU REALIZE IT OR NOT, YOU ALREADY HAVE A MESSAGE ABOUT SEX RESTING IN THE CORE OF YOUR UNDERSTANDING

As we began to talk about this topic of God and sex, we must first realize that it is impossible for us to learn about sex without knowing where we have already learned about it. Why? I can teach you new ideas, theology, and scientific statistics until my nose bleeds, but if you're already indoctrinated, you've already made up your mind on the matter. Chances are that you won't be able to fully hear what I have to say with an open mind because you're hearing it through the filter of what you know or what you've experienced.

Whether you realize it or not, you already have a message about sex resting in the core of your understanding. It might have been a verbal message at home; it might have been an environment where the silence spoke louder than words.

Needless to say, we've all learned something about it. For some of us, it was a solid, healthy foundation that is ready to be built on. For others, well, not so much. This is why it's crucial to go back to the beginning — our beginning — to see what was written on the bark of our own personal little tree of knowledge.

What's Behind Door Number 1: Silence

We've come to find that there are three main environments in which we learn about sex. The first environment we will refer to is a "Silent Environment".

Imagine a bedroom door. The door is locked, it has been locked for most of your life, and someone threw away the key. All of the other rooms in your life — kitchen, living room, bathroom — are accessible to you. The bedroom door, however, is shut. It's almost like it doesn't even exist. What's behind that door? A big, whirling black hole of mystery.

Your parents never mentioned anything to you. Your church has no idea what you're talking about. "What door? We don't see a door."

This is the silent environment.

This is a very unique environment — it's where we learn that sex is neither good nor bad, it's just never talked about. You begin to wonder what the big deal is. The people in your life never told you anything and you were left to figure it out on your own. For most of us, that meant watching movies, staying up to watch late night TV, browsing the Internet, or asking friends. Maybe you were surprised one day to find that there was a whole world out there no one told you about. Perhaps it was overwhelming. Maybe you happened to be in a situation, even physically, where you didn't know what was going on. It just happened and you suddenly realized that there was more to this than meets the eye.

The interesting issue dwells in the fact that silence is the only voice you cannot correct. How can you correct something that hasn't been said? The question now is this: what is silence saying?

SILENCE IS THE ONLY VOICE YOU CANNOT CORRECT

It's fascinating to think about the silent environment because in the midst of living life, we're distracted by the silent noise of the unknown; the curiosity of ourselves and those around us is often too much to bear. As a result of this environment, we learn that sex is a part of life, but it's too private to talk about or it's not overly important. After all, if it was really that important, someone would have said something. If it was really vital to know what it's meant to be, how it's meant to be used, and the power of it, then the most important people in our lives would have talked to us about it, right? Our parents thought they were protecting us, or perhaps they really didn't think it was important, either. Whatever the case was, that silence said something to you about its value, its importance and its power.

Contrary to popular belief, the silent environment is not the most pure environment. Sex must be talked about; if we don't, the silence we believe will protect us actually opens a door, and we often see shame, guilt, confusion and fear file right in to fill in the gaps of the unsaid, particularly in the lives of children and youth. If time is not given to explain the value of something, we're left to discover and learn about it on our own.

CONTRARY TO POPULAR BELIEF, THE SILENT ENVIRONMENT IS NOT THE MOST PURE ENVIRONMENT

If we go through this process alone, we decide to go with whatever suits us or whatever sounds good for the moment. The danger is this: when we're not informed by people we trust, we let other voices influence our perspective. We begin to learn about sex, sexuality and beauty from pop culture. Society begins to dictate what we should do with our bodies or what should happen in our relationships. These ideas become our beliefs.

It all changes now. Let's break the silence.

What's Behind Door Number 2: SATU- RATED

The second environment that we find — one that we see the most in our contemporary culture — is what we like to call a "Saturated Environment".

In this scenario, imagine a bedroom door that is completely open — almost as if there's no door at all. Everything is accessible, nothing is hidden, and there's no indication that there's anything sacred or special happening in that open room. Those around you talk about sex through crude jokes, watch explicit movies with sex scenes, and have casual, overt sexual relationships. If this was your home environment, you probably can't remember having a deep or intentional "sex talk", and why would you need to? It was just everywhere.

Sex was, simply put, a part of life. You learned that it's okay to view sex as nothing more than a casual physical experience — anything more is over-thinking a simple encounter.

Many who came from this environment don't understand why sex is such a big deal to other people.

"What's so sacred about it? I don't sense that there's any kind of spirit/soul connection to the act itself. It's just a way of connecting on a physical level and showing someone you love them. Right?"

Without a door to the bedroom everyone in the house can see every detail of what's going on. Sex loses its mystery, its sacredness. It becomes casual and familiar, something we throw in with our everyday activities. In fact, everyone becomes so familiar with sex that they think, "What more is there to learn? I already know it all. I've seen it, been around it, had my own experiences. What else do I need to know?"

Here lies the deception that occurs in this over-saturated environment — Since it's everywhere, we are comfortable with it. No shame, no blame, no guilt. All good. Or is it?

The world paints this picture so clearly, doesn't it? We turn on the TV and watch sitcoms that celebrate one-night stands and "friends with benefits", suggesting that this is just a part of life. So what? You get naked, you fool around. It doesn't matter. It's your body, so you can do whatever you want with it as long as everyone is consenting. I made no commitment to you, you made no commitment to me. What's the big deal?

> **WITHOUT A DOOR TO THE BEDROOM, EVERYONE IN THE HOUSE CAN SEE EVERY DETAIL OF WHAT'S GOING ON**

When we live out of these misguided beliefs, we are violating our nature and design. We believe that we are powerful individuals, choosing how to use our bodies. However, we can't stop our bodies from doing what they were created to do, and, consequently, many of us think that there's something wrong with us. For example, the lingering feelings toward someone that you can't get over — feelings of jealousy, sense of ownership, feeling bonded — throw us for a loop because we think we should be able to have an encounter and walk away. We feel that we should be able to give away the most precious part of us without any commitment, and then just move on with life.

There is a generation on the earth today that believes they should be able to walk away from a sexual encounter (or romantic relationship) without it affecting them at all. The truth is that we were built to bond for a lifetime, not separate after each encounter.

> **THE TRUTH IS THAT WE WERE BUILT TO BOND FOR A LIFETIME, NOT SEPARATE AFTER EACH ENCOUNTER**

We've made something sacred into something casual; something holistic into something basic. Is this the result of an over-saturated culture?

We must understand one thing when it comes to this environment: the saturated environment is not the healthiest environment when it comes to learning about sex. Experience doesn't lead us to freedom, wisdom does. Making something an everyday part of life may allow us to become more comfortable, but it will not give us the full, whole picture of what God designed that we require for a healthy perspective.

If you were raised in this environment, give us a chance to show you how your spirit and soul are touched by sexual activity. We hope that you'll have a greater understanding of yourself and that it will bring freedom and light into your life.

What's Behind Door Number 3: CONFLICTED

The third environment that we find is what we call the "Conflicted Environment."

Imagine a bedroom door that swings open and closed. You get a glimpse of something — an idea, an experience — but before you can figure out what's going on, the door closes. We see this happen a lot in the church. We're told, "Once you're married, you get full access to whatever is behind there. However, before that day comes, you shouldn't even want to look inside. If you do, for shame! Shame on you for even wanting to know what's inside of there, you little pervert."

Then, once you're married, the door swings wide open and the message changes to, "It's going to be amazing! Once you get through that door, it will be unbelievable. Euphoric. You're not just marrying a person, you're marrying a sex slave. They're going to do everything you've ever imagined. Buckle up, baby, it's going to be the ride of your life! Don't worry — you'll know what to do once you get there."

"But hey, you're not married yet. You just stay pure and don't look in there because God forbid you get a glimpse of something you can't have, lest you succumb to temptation."

SEX IS A LANGUAGE, NOT JUST AN EXPERIENCE OF PLEASURE

In this environment, we may feel like we're living a double life. We want to be pure, but we peek through the door because we have thoughts, desires, and hair growing in new places; we're being drawn by a natural curiosity about ourselves and others. We feel shame, and yet the desire to know more is insatiable. As we white-knuckle it to our wedding night, we begin to dream up and cling to unrealistic expectations about what sex will be. Unfortunately, while the "hope" we have for sex may help us stay pure in the waiting, it can lead us into unforeseeable disappointment and pain if we're not careful.

The conflict classically arises when we get married and walk through the door, only to realize that sex does not start as a magical, euphoric experience. We are taken aback, confused and hurt that it wasn't everything we were told it would be. Sometimes there is even shame involved, particularly for women, who have to make a sudden transition from sex being "bad" or "forbidden" to "good" and "expected".

As you can see, this environment, even with its celebration of virginity and married-sex, doesn't fully translate the reality of sex. Sex is a language, not just an experience of pleasure. We learn to give and take within this secret world where a private connection is taking place — our bodies and souls are building memories, creating bonds and being knit together. All of this takes time to grow into — not just sex itself, but yourself and your spouse: body, soul and spirit. It is a life-long learning adventure, not of a series of one night stands.

In this conflicted environment, the kind of inner monologue we hear is, "I'm just going to try to do what I'm supposed to do, and hopefully I don't mess it all up." How many of us have heard something similar to this in the church? "Do it this way. Why? Because it's the right way." Our response to this teaching is, "I want to be pure because I need to be pure,"

Although it's beautiful to have that desire, it's not enough. We must know why we want and need this in order to be healthy and live purely. The white-knuckle approach to purity may control behaviors, but it can't resolve a heart condition or change a belief system. Striving starts when we operate out of rules without understanding the love and purpose behind them. When we pursue any ideal outside of love, we will never produce fruit that remains. This is why so many of just want to pray away our sex drives and escape the growing process altogether; it's too hard to try to do it on our own.

When God gave you your sex drive, He had a plan. He knew that it would take self-control and patience to manage. He knew it would require you to grow in all of the other fruits of the Spirit as well — love for yourself, joy and peace in the waiting, kindness toward yourself and others, good choices, and faithfulness as you trust in Him. He knew that you wouldn't be able to do it without His help. And He said it was good.

In giving you your sex drive, God had a plan to grow you up, both in maturity and relationship with Him. Because He started this good work in you, He will be faithful to see it completed. He is not going to leave you until you figure out how to be perfect. He is going to teach you how to steward it in such a way that honors Him as well as the person you will eventually commit to for the rest of your life. No matter how hard you pray for it to leave, He won't take it away; it was a gift!

So, what are we supposed to do about it? My suggestion is to open the door and look in. Not with shame, not with the guilt that comes when we feel we're perverted, but take a healthy glimpse inside for the sake of understanding. God opened the door long ago and it was the church that shut it, not Him. He always wanted to show us exactly what sex was meant to be, and He wanted us to know the power of sex. He wanted us to be fully aware and fully alive, and fully connected with our spouse without the regret, shame or pain that attaches to the pure thing that God created.

So again, the three environments are the Silent Environment, Saturated Environment and the Conflicted Environment. Which do you think was God's plan for us? Do you think God had a door in the garden somewhere that swung open and closed? How about the Israelites — did they blush when the blood covered sheet was thrown over the bridal chamber wall? (If you don't know what I'm talking about, skip to Part 5.)

It's safe to say that none of these environments are completely ideal; none of them were what God intended for us. Luckily, there are many ways to overcome what we've learned from them. Think for a moment about which environment seems to be closest to the one you experienced growing up. What was said to you? As we go into this topic of sexuality, what areas do you feel uncomfortable with? Or overly confident about? Keep in touch with how you're feeling. If you think to yourself that you don't want to talk about something, or that we're making a big deal out of something, or that the church shouldn't be talking about it, etc., pause and try to connect with where those thoughts are coming from. Then go to work on renewing your mind by replacing those old beliefs with God's truth.

As we go on this journey together, allow God to redefine your understanding. Lean into the garden, into the place where He said, "I made it and I said it was good." Our goal is that you finish this book feeling freer, more confident, and more informed

IN ORDER TO CHANGE CULTURE, WE MUST CHANGE OURSELVES FIRST

than when you opened it. And we want this educated, whole, powerful you to have fulfilling relationships and marriages. At the end of everything, we all want healthy families, don't we? We want to have the most beautiful, powerful marriages the world has ever seen. We want the people who have come from brokenness to arrive at a place where they are whole and healthy, happy in their journey, feeling fulfilled with what God has for them.

This is what it's all about. It's about a revolution. Whatever we've experienced, we must be able to say that we want to think differently about sexuality. In order to change culture, we must change ourselves first. We need to be willing to go to the places that have never been looked at with honesty and openness so that God can define this for us. We want a moral revolution. We want purity and holiness to move upon the face of the earth until all people are free and fully alive, knowing how to manage and steward their sexuality, their desires and their choices in such a way that it brings glory to God.

You know what? I think it's possible. I know it's possible because it's happened in my life and it's happening with people in our community. I've watched countless individuals, couples and families walk out of abuse, addiction, pain, and all kinds of darkness, completely redeemed and restored, as though it never happened. That's the power of God for all who believe. And He can do the same for you, no matter what your story is.

④ LIES, LIES, EVERYWHERE

Before we jump into our comprehensive exploration of sexuality (all that good stuff), we first want to address our belief systems. This is important because what we believe, we live out. It doesn't matter what we say about sex — what you believe to be true, at the core of your being, is what you're going to live out. We can fill this book with great information (which we have) but once you walk away, you'll do what's inside of you. So, we want to take some time and make sure that you've got a solid foundation of truth that you can build your life upon. In this chapter, we're going to start with some beliefs we might have about God, Himself.

> **IF WE ARE GOING TO TRUST WHAT GOD HAS TO SAY ABOUT SEX, WE FIRST HAVE TO TRUST HIM**

Here's the deal— If we are going to trust what God has to say about sex, we first have to trust Him. You see, it's difficult to trust an opinion without understanding the motives behind it. You will always question what you are asked to do, if you don't know that the person asking has your good in mind. In the same way, we need to understand God's character —that He honest, faithful, loving, and all kinds of good — before we can trust or embrace what He's asking us to do.

If we don't believe that God's intentions toward us are good, pure and kind, then we will poke holes in whatever He (or our church) asks us to do. We'll say, "Sure, it sounds good in theory, but I don't know if that's realistic. I know you're telling me to wait, but am I going to get all my needs met? Are you going to take care of me? Are you really that good?" These are the lies that affect our ability to see sex in a good, healthy way. They affect our ability to see God as who He truly is. In order to fill you with the truth, we'll need to rid you of the lies that are blocking your tunnels of living water.

Lie #1: God can reject us

I have seen this lie in action, time and time again. I will watch people try to do what's right. They'll say something like, "God, I'm yours. I want to do what you want me to do." Then, moments later they'll mess it all up. They'll go and do the exact opposite. Sometimes they'll completely blow up their lives. You know, they get into that relationship they should never have gotten into, or hang out with the wrong person, or do something they shouldn't have done. Why? Are they just sinners? Are they even saved? Don't they love God?

Let me decode something for you: when we believe that God can reject us, we will run from Him, instead of to Him. Why? Because we believe we must be perfect before He will relate with us. When we always feel rejected by God, we turn to other things to make us feel loved, safe, powerful, fulfilled, or satisfied. We will also try to hide from Him. When Adam and Eve did what was wrong, and believed they were in trouble, what did they do? They sewed leaves and made outfits. They hid. (I don't know about you but I'd love to see those. When I get to heaven I'm going to ask to see those outfits. Was it a bikini or a one-piece for Eve? A little speedo for Adam? I bet they were good!)

When we believe that God can reject us, we begin to pull away from Him to protect ourselves. It is our human nature to put a wall up when someone hurts us; we don't like pain. When we don't trust someone, we don't give them access to us. It's a relational rejection. We don't necessarily believe that God is kicking us out of heaven, but that He just can't be near us right now. So, instead of being rejected, we reject God — first. Of course, no one is going to come out and say it — we'll all say that God loves us and is for us— but inside we know that there are parts of us that believe that God rejects us when we mess up.

Let's use a practical example. Do you own a cell phone? I'll just assume that the answer is yes. How many of us, when we're angry with someone, deny an incoming call? How many of you love pressing that silence button whenever you decide to ignore someone? Come on, I know some of you do. There's a sense of power that comes when we can deny someone, right? Some of us take pride in that moment, saying, "I'm not taking that call. You're not going to talk to me right now. I'll talk to you when I'm good and ready." What does this have to do with God? Unfortunately, many of us believe that God is like that with us. It's as if when we're saying, "God I love you!", He pushes the silence button.

"Denied!" He shouts smugly. "Angels did you see that? It's going to take ten more worship services and some consistent tithing before I'm going to pick up that call."

There's a lie that tells us He turns away from us in His anger. We think this because somewhere in us we believe that God couldn't look at Jesus on the cross. We think that He can't stand to look at us in sin.

The danger is this — if we believe that God can reject us, we put ourselves in a little purgatory. God cannot get His love to us because we'll ignore it until we feel like we deserve love again. This is because we think He wants to punish us for our disobedience. It's important to realize that He doesn't put us in these places; we put ourselves there. When we embrace a lie as truth, we shroud ourselves with a veil that clouds our understanding of God's true nature.

The truth is this: God will not reject you. He is not afraid of your sin. He will not refuse to have relationship with you just because you're not perfect. The truth is the nature of God is unconditional love. He is slow to anger and His mercies are new every morning.

GOD WILL NOT REJECT YOU. HE IS NOT AFRAID OF YOUR SIN

He's the best dad, the best mom, you could ever imagine. To be frank, He would have to reject Himself in order to reject you. Through Jesus, the new covenant says that by grace we are saved, and there's nothing that could separate us from His love.

In reality, we have the same nature as Adam and Eve. It isn't unnatural to want to hide from God when we've messed up, but it also isn't grounded in the perfect love that casts out all fear. We must remember the next part of the story that says it was God who came and looked for them. When they did what was wrong, He didn't sit on His throne, waiting for them to repent. He went looking for them, and called for them. If God did not relationally reject Adam and Eve, He's not going to reject you. In the Message Bible, Romans 8:31–39 says this:

" *The One who died for us — the one who was raised to life for us — is in the presence of God this very moment sticking up for us. Do you think anyone is going to be able to drive a wedge between us and Christ's love for us? There is no way! Not trouble, not hard times, not hatred, not hunger, not homelessness, not bullying threats, not backstabbing, not even the worst sins listed in scripture.* **"**

> **WHEREVER YOU ARE RIGHT NOW, HE IS PLEADING FOR YOU TO COME AND BE CLOSE WITH HIM**

Wherever you are right now, He is pleading for you to come and be close with Him. Nothing will keep you from His love. It's time to come out of hiding, take off the fig leaves, and face the One who is, and always will be, for you.

Lie #2: God can ignore us

When we buy into this lie, we don't believe that God will outright reject us, but we do believe that He will ignore us. It's something in us that believes that when we talk to God, He's like that friend who's always on their smart phone. The one who is all, "Mmhmm. Uh huh, sure.. Yep. Sorry, what?" when you're trying to have a conversation with them. It's like this: "Hey God. God, I just want to talk to you about my purity. Can we fix this? I think I messed up there. Hey, God?"

"Just a minute," He says, without looking up from His phone, "I'll get right back to you on that. Just trying to save Africa right now. Uh huh, just a minute. Oh look — your pure and righteous bestie is in trouble. BRB."

How many of us truly think that God ignores us in order to make us figure things out on our own? So that we can become stronger people? Or He disconnects when it doesn't seem like we're doing things one hundred percent right?

It's dangerous to think this because when we feel He's disconnected, we think He can't see us. Then we believe that we can do things that we otherwise wouldn't do because it doesn't matter; He's not really looking at us anyway. But it does matter. He is with us, His gaze is upon us, and the truth is you can't surprise God. He does not disconnect from you, He's not afraid of sin, and He doesn't run from it. God is not impulsive. He's not like your parents who might have been impulsive. I know that for me, I had to learn that God's nature is vastly different from that of my parent's. Whenever something bad was happening I would think, "If mom's home, I will tell her. If dad's home… I'll pray about it!" God, on the other hand, is entirely patient with us and does not respond in an irrational, emotional way. Psalm 103 says: "The Lord is compassionate and gracious, slow to anger, abounding in love."

When it comes to your sexuality, your desires, and your thoughts, He's not impatiently waiting for you to get your act together. But many of us believe that God is angry and that His anger is going to move us to repentance. Again, looking at scripture, we know that isn't true. Romans 2:4 says, "Don't you know it's His kindness that leads you to repentance?"

The truth is that in the midst of our weakness, God is loving us, showing kindness, and strengthening us. He entreats us into who He is, saying, "My grace is all you need. My power works best in weakness" (2 Corinthians 12:9, NLT). Paul says that we can actually boast in our weakness, so that Christ is glorified through moving in us.

> **THE TRUTH IS THAT IN THE MIDST OF OUR WEAKNESS, GOD IS LOVING US, SHOWING KINDNESS, AND STRENGTHENING US**

We get a do-over with God. It doesn't matter what you've done, who you've been raised by, who you've been out with or what you've been watching. It doesn't matter what you're doing behind closed doors or even in wide open places in front of everyone. At the end of the day, we all get another chance.

Lie #3: God can withhold from us

This last lie, I believe, can be the most dangerous one. It's so subtle that it will keep even the best of us from the vibrant, abundant life Jesus bought for us. It doesn't matter how godly, god-fearing or loving we are, this lie is so sly that it will grab a hold of people without them knowing. Read carefully; many of us won't realize that it's living on the inside of us, causing us to miss out on so many opportunities and blessings.

Let me illustrate this for you. Let's say there's a big pie in front of you and it represents God's will for your life. You were born again, you did everything right, you memorized scripture, you worshipped when you should, and went to school. When you did something wrong, you repented quickly. We have a picture of what the "good Christian life" is supposed to look like. After everything, if we do everything the way we're supposed to, we will get the whole pie.

But what if we don't do everything right? There is a feeling deep inside that tells us that we'll only get a portion of the pie. There's a part of us that believes that we only get what we deserve. Isn't that what the world is saying to us? You get a promotion because you earned it. You get an amazing family because you worked hard. You get a nice retirement because you slaved for years. As much as there's truth in all of that, God doesn't function this way.

Whether we're not virgins anymore, already divorced, still addicted to something, or perhaps we feel we're not fully pure yet, Jesus paid for it all. He has made a way for us to get everything that He deserves. Unfortunately, we still think that if we had done everything right, worked hard, saved ourselves, we would have received the whole thing. Our expectations are incredibly low, and many of us tell ourselves, "Just be happy with the piece you got. You could have had nothing, after all." Some people go as far to suggest that these burdens, or areas of lack, are their cross to bear or the thorn in their side.

Whatever the case may be, this all smells like a lie: the lie that says God will actually withhold His fullness and abundance from us. It says that His goodness is dependent on us. Nothing could be further from the truth.

The truth is that it's just not in His nature to do that. Even in the story of the prodigal son, the disobedient son came home to open arms and a fatted calf killed for the occasion. No, the prodigal son didn't get what he deserved, and neither will you. The ultimate truth, and the beauty of what Jesus has done, is that you are worthy to receive it all. Jesus paid the price for our sins on the cross so that we wouldn't get what we deserved — we would get what He deserved. To think anything less is to think that what He did wasn't enough.

God will not withhold from us. He doesn't hold our past against us. He loves us and it's not in His nature to play favorites. He sees us all the same, and He will give us the very best if we want it. When it comes to our sexuality, whether we've messed up or been abused, none of the past will be held against us when it comes to God's perfect will over us to live in abundance and freedom. It's time to start living like we believe that. Don't you think?

> **GOD WILL NOT WITHHOLD FROM US. HE DOESN'T HOLD OUR PAST AGAINST US**

02 SEX And IDENTITY

Too often we try to be a "human doing" before we have become a "human being."

JOHN C. MAXWELL

⑤ I.D., PLEASE

The Bible says that what we believe, we live out (2 Corinthians 5:7). This is true in every area of life. If you've ever trained as an athlete, chances are your coach had you practice visualization. When you visualize, you play a scenario over in your head — the sights, sounds, textures, stance, technique — everything that you'd need to do to make the perfect free-throw, mogul run, or knock-out punch.

ANYTHING IS POSSIBLE IF A PERSON BELIEVES

But what makes it work? It's believing it. It's being convinced that it is possible in real life. If you can believe it, you can be it. The Bible said it like this: "Anything is possible if a person believes" (Mark 9:23, NLT).

Just saying you believe something is not enough. We can say that we value and believe in healthy living, but as we eat our third piece of cheesecake in one sitting, it might become evident that this isn't the case. What you do shows what you value; what you live out is really what you believe.

For example, some people believe that family is very important, and so they choose to work jobs that allow them to spend evenings with their families. Some trust (believe) God will bring them the perfect spouse at the right time, so they wait patiently instead of frantically serial-dating to find the one. Some believe they are not worth loving and, consequently, don't value themselves. Many of these people spend their lives sabotaging their relationships and pushing people away. They're all becoming what they believe.

Many of us in the church say that we are children of God, heirs, chosen and dearly loved, but how many really believe it? Where is the fruit to prove it? Where is our confidence, peace, love, patience, strength and holiness? In Matthew 5:48 Jesus said, "Be perfect, just as your Father in heaven in perfect." Did He say this to discourage us? To remind us that we'll always fall short? Was He barking a military order to whip us into shape?

What if He said it because He wants us to believe it is possible — that we can actually be perfect, pure, and holy, like the One in whose image we were created — so we can become it? If we don't believe we are who God says we are, we'll never walk in our full identity as God's children. But when we do, He becomes our Father, and we leave behind slavery for son-ship and daughter-ship. We no longer act like orphans, unable to trust, but learn to yield to a loving Father who wants to love, guide and protect us.

In case you've never thought much about your identity, specifically who God says you are, here are some thoughts to consider. All of these truths show an aspect of who you are, and hold power that will shape you into who you will become. Place these truths in front of you on a daily basis until you believe them and start to live them out. Some people like to put a note on their mirror or car dashboard, or read them aloud.

I am chosen.

Ephesians 1:5 says, *"He destined us to be adopted as His children through the covenant Jesus the Anointed inaugurated in His sacrificial life. This was His pleasure and His will for us."* (VOICE)

This means that I am never rejected or abandoned and I will never go without. He wanted me before I ever wanted Him. He loves me and also likes me. It brings Him great pleasure to have me in His family.

I am a child and heir of God.

Romans 8:17 says, *"God's Spirit touches our spirits and confirms who we really are. We know who he is, and we know who we are: Father and children. And we know we are going to get what's coming to us — an unbelievable inheritance!"* (MSG)

This means that I belong to Him. I am accepted and significant. I am a part of His family and He is proud to call me His! There are more incredible gifts and surprises coming in my lifetime than I could ever imagine.

I am loved.

Romans 8:35 says, *"So who can separate us? What can come between us and the love of God's Anointed? Can troubles, hardships, persecution, hunger, poverty, danger, or even death? The answer is, absolutely nothing."* (VOICE)

This means that I am inseparable from the love of God. No matter what happens, I belong to Him and with Him. No sin or mistake is too big to keep me away from His love, help and healing. What do I have to be afraid of? Nothing! He protects and champions me.

I am perfect in Jesus' eyes.

2 Corinthians 5:21 says, *"For God made Christ, who never sinned, to be the offering for our sin so that we could be made right with God through Christ." (NLT)*

This means that I am in right standing with God. I don't have to earn holiness, because I am already holy and set apart because of what Jesus did. I am righteous. I have been washed clean. I am pure!

I am a saint.

Romans 7:4–6 says, *"So, my dear brothers and sisters, this is the point: You died to the power of the law when you died with Christ. And now you are united with the one who was raised from the dead. As a result, we can produce a harvest of good deeds for God. When we were controlled by our old nature, sinful desires were at work within us, and the law aroused these evil desires that produced a harvest of sinful deeds, resulting in death. But now we have been released from the law, for we died to it and are no longer captive to its power. Now we can serve God, not in the old way of obeying the letter of the law, but in the new way of living in the Spirit." (MSG)*

This means that I am no longer a sinner in God's eyes. It is now in my nature to do good, not evil. I can live confidently, knowing that I can walk daily in His will knowing I am in right standing before God.

I am not who I used to be;

I am a new person.

2 Corinthians 5:17 says, *"This means that anyone who belongs to Christ has become a new person. The old life is gone; a new life has begun!" (NLT).*

This means that my past does not define me. In God's eyes, the person I used to be is dead and buried. My past decision will not define my future success. I have a new life and I can live it to the fullest. I have a clean slate and a world full of possibilities.

⑥ POWER TO THE PEOPLE

Remember when I said that what we believe, we will live out? At the beginning of this chapter, we talked about how our beliefs shape our lives. In this section, I want to give you 5 Power Beliefs — five foundational truths that are keys to helping you make good choices with your sexuality. They will illuminate your world and help you live fully alive. These truths must be central in your core beliefs if you are going to live the life God intended for you to live.

Healthy beliefs are like headlights that help us see as we drive in dark places; Psalm 119 tells us God's truths help us navigate even the most treacherous territory and stay on track. If you don't have these five beliefs already, you may have a headlight out, so to speak. There may be parts of your life that are still blurred or dim, preventing you from seeing God and yourself in truth. You may even feel powerless, stuck or discouraged. You may feel depressed or hopeless about relationships. You may have lost your peace. Whatever situation you're in, don't despair; the truth is on the way. You can get your power back, starting now. Let us examine these beliefs together.

POWER BELIEF #1

Our first power belief is that **I believe God.**

HIS WORDS ARE LIFE AND HIS PROMISES ARE TRUE. THIS MEANS IF HE SAID IT, HE'S GOING TO DO IT

Do we really believe God? The Bible says that God is Truth and it's one of His names (John 14:6) which means God doesn't lie to us. He doesn't tell us half-truths, or the truth sometimes, and little white lies later. He's not hiding truth. He is truth. His words are life and His promises are true. This means if He said it, He's going to do it. That's the God we serve. If He said, "Be pure because I am pure," it's because we have the grace to do it. If we do what He asks of us, we get to live a fully illuminated life as was intended.

The ability to live as you were created is to live with freedom and influence. When you use something as it was intended, it's very powerful. When you don't, then you don't have its full capacity. It's like staying in first gear and never getting to fourth gear. These power beliefs are designed to kick you into high gear and help you to run at your full capacity in Christ.

Why is this important when it comes to sex? If you don't believe God's promises, part of you might take control of the reigns when it comes to your sexuality. You might think you'll do a better job because you don't believe He'll help you get your needs met. You might not trust that God knows what kind of man or woman you want. You don't get it God, so because you don't get it I'm going to stand over here like an orphan and I'm going to feel alone because you don't have what I need. Yes, that's what it sounds like.

This, my friends, is the greatest lie of the enemy. We all know what happened in the garden. That's what the serpent told Adam and Eve: "Don't believe God — He lied to you. He's hiding something from you." When we believe those lies, we start to give in to those voices that tell us that God is not entirely trustworthy.

Remember, the enemy only had to tell a half-lie to get them to believe the whole lie. Just a half-lie. The enemy won't just say, "God's not going to give you happiness" or "God hates you." He's just going to say, "I don't think that God's going to work it out; I don't think you're ever going to be that happy. You've waited a long time, haven't you? Maybe you should make something happen on your own. Can God really be that good if He's let you go through all this?"

If we believe God is who He says He is, and He does what He says He is going to do, we don't have a reason to fear. We never have a reason to control. We don't need to strive or even manipulate. We never have to live with anxiety, depression or hopelessness. We can lean into a Father. A Father who is Comfort, Protection, Provider, Healer, Redeemer (among many other things). We can know that He will take care of it all, even when we don't understand.

> **IF WE BELIEVE GOD IS WHO HE SAYS HE IS, AND HE DOES WHAT HE SAYS HE IS GOING TO DO, WE DON'T HAVE A REASON TO FEAR**

We must believe God on the inside, no matter what we are experiencing on the outside. The Bible says that what we believe, we will see. Believing you are pure because of Him, not because of you. Believing your future is full of love, comfort, intimacy and connection. Believing it's important to give our sexuality to God before "that someone" comes around so our motives are good and our hearts are in the right place. Not doing it for anyone else. Doing it for Him, and doing it for yourself because you are no longer an orphan, but a child of a really good Father.

POWER BELIEF #2

Our second power belief is that **I trust God.**

God is trustworthy. He's always the same, He's all knowing and all understanding. He will always give His best and He will never leave our side. This fundamental truth is illustrated beautifully throughout scripture for us. In 2 Samuel 7:28 it says, "Now, O Lord God, you are God, and your words are truth, and you have promised this good thing to Your servant." King David understands something about God that allows him to put his trust in Him: His word is true. Psalm 125:1 says, "Those who trust in the LORD are as Mount Zion, which cannot be moved, but abides forever." We can firmly place ourselves in the belief that God makes us strong, secure, and steadfast. We need only to put our trust in Him.

I remember a time when this was illustrated to me perfectly. We were planning a trip to Disneyland with our four boys and my oldest, Judah, wanted to save up money for the trip.

I told Judah that I would give him one dollar for every chore completed. So, Judah immediately went to work vacuuming, raking the yard and emptying the dishwasher. After a couple of months, he had earned fourteen dollars. This may not seem like a lot, but to any six year old, that's a lot of money. Not to mention it was a whole fourteen dollars more than any of his brothers had, so that's something to be proud of.

The big day finally arrived, and it also happened to be our second oldest son's birthday. Hudson wasn't really going to get any gifts because his gift was Disneyland. (Actually, it's his gift for the next ten years because that's how much it costs to go to Disneyland. He doesn't know that. Don't tell him.)

When we were all bundled into the car, we gave Hudson his one gift — a card from his grandparents. He opened it up, and what do you think was inside? A twenty dollar bill. Hudson is elated. He's doing the happy dance. "I HAVE

TWENTY DOLLARS! I'm going to Disneyland, I'm so excited!" We are all rejoicing with Hudson, saying, "That's incredible! That's awesome, I can't believe it!"

I then realize what else is happening in the car. I turn my attention to Judah, who now has his arms folded across his chest and has huge crocodile tears sitting in his eyes, which begin to roll down his face.

"Judah. How are you doing, buddy?"

"I only got fourteen dollars and Hudson has twenty!" he let's out with a sob of emotion.

Inside I'm thinking, "Guys, it's fourteen dollars. You're only going to be able to buy a hot dog in Disneyland. Maybe a side of fries. Maybe. It's not a lot of money."

I'm having this moment when all of a sudden I look at Judah and say something I did not expect to hear. I look at Judah right in the eyes and say clearly:

"Judah. You are not going to go without. Judah. You are not going to go without. Judah. You are not going to go without. You're going to be okay."

As I say it, I hear God say to me: That's exactly what I'm saying to you, Havilah. Trust me. You will not go without.

I realized that we are all going to have twenty dollar moments in our lives. It's the moment we didn't earn, the moment where God is kind and gives us a blessing greater than you imagined. But most days are fourteen dollar days; we do our best, working and being diligent with what's in front of us, sometimes with minimal results.

WE ARE ALL GOING TO HAVE TWENTY DOLLAR MOMENTS IN OUR LIVES

On those days God says, I will sustain you for the season you're in. Trust me. You will not go without.

Every moment is an opportunity to put our trust in God's intentions for us. His plans are good, and His ability to work it out on our behalf is better. His time frame isn't always what we would think is ideal, but it is what we need.

What we tend to do is look at another person's $20 moment and judge them. We think that we deserve it more than them. We're working hard, we're cute, we're working out. We compare ourselves to them, thinking things like:

Why does that guy get a girl like that? How did she get married so fast? I'm way cuter than her! That girl gets a guy and is walking down the aisle faster than I can say hello. What's going on? I stayed pure!

That divorced guy walks into our church and suddenly gets the girl every guy has been trying to marry! This is not fair!

We think that they are getting blessed and we're not. But the truth is this — there's plenty of blessing to go around. It's just that they are having their twenty dollar moment and we are not. The moment we start looking at someone's twenty dollar bill is the moment we take our eyes off of what God is doing in our lives. Comparison is the enemy's way of telling you God cheated you. If we start to think that what we have isn't enough, we won't see what God has for us in the season we're in.

You will not go without.

So, what's going on? Well, maybe it's not time for you to fall in love yet. Maybe it will hurt you more than help you. We must look at other people's lives as separate from ourselves. We can celebrate them without losing to them. Say to yourself, God has a twenty dollar moment for me. It may not be today but it's coming. God gives good gifts to His kids and — good news — you're one of His kids. It may take a little time, but in the meantime, be okay with your fourteen dollars. You're working hard, growing in strength and endurance, and you're allowing yourself to trust God. When He wants to give you your twenty dollar moment, He will give it to you.

What does this have to do with sex? A great number of us tend to act out in anxiety when we think our needs won't be met. This means that many of us don't fully trust God. We're afraid that we're not going to be loved, we're not going to be picked, or we're not going to be seen. We think that no one can end our loneliness, or soothe our pain, so we look at porn and meet that need quickly. Or we wear provocative outfits to get the attention we desire. We want to feel powerful and in control. We can look at something, or display ourselves, and get our sexual needs met quickly without it really costing anything. What we don't know is that it is costing us, and we're going to miss our twenty dollar moment living that way. We're going spiritually bankrupt because we don't trust God.

In order to be powerful in your sexuality, you must be willing to give God your life, surrender your future, and put your trust in Him completely. What He's going to do for you is so much better than what you can do for yourself.

POWER BELIEF #3

Our third power belief is that **I am powerful.**

We are powerful. Sometimes when I say this, I get met with slight opposition. People have often said to me, "I don't think that we're powerful. Only the Holy Spirit makes us powerful."

It's true. The Holy Spirit does give us power, love and a sound mind. However, the Bible also says the power of life and death are in our tongues. Our ability to choose Heaven or Hell makes us powerful. Our ability to choose to turn the other cheek with our enemies makes us powerful. The ability to choose to be who God has called you to be makes you powerful! You're so powerful, in fact, that God left the choice up to you, and He's not going to manipulate you or pull it away

> **IN THE BEGINNING HE GAVE US SOMETHING CALLED A FREE WILL, AND HE'S NOT ABOUT TO TAKE IT AWAY FROM US**

from you. In the beginning He gave us something called a free will, and He's not about to take it away from us.

Let us work to gain an understanding of how powerful we really are. We must not be deceived in thinking that a sexual encounter isn't a big deal. The memories will be held in your body and in theirs. Your mind is very powerful and what you choose to do, your body will follow. As we begin to renew our minds — as is discussed in Romans 12 — our bodies will begin to follow because that's how we were created to be. If you don't feel very powerful yet, don't worry. When we choose to be powerful and choose the way of life, a supernatural ability comes over us to do what's right even when we don't feel that we have it naturally.

Yes, let us not forget or diminish the influence the Spirit has over our abilities. As much as we are strong, the Spirit gives us a power unlike any other. Philippians 4:13 says that you can do all things through Christ who strengthens you. There's another version that says you are equal to anything that you face. Not out of your own might, but through the Spirit of God that is in you, no matter what is happening around you or what you believe. At this very moment when you ask Jesus and the Holy Spirit to come within you, you are actually asking God to demonstrate to you that you can live in power.

We are also responsible for our choices in which dwells the power for us to change or remain the same. When we decide to serve God and surrender our lives to Him, we receive a power that enables us to change everything. Even though circumstances might have been against us, we get to choose to act differently and take responsibility. He anoints us to operate within the parameters of wisdom and responsibility.

He rewards our integrity and our obedience. He gives us grace when we choose what's right.

> **WHEN YOU BELIEVE SOMEONE ELSE CAN CONTROL YOU, YOU WILL LIVE AN "OUT OF CONTROL" LIFE**

When you believe someone else can control you, you will live an "out of control" life. When you think that somebody else can control your sexuality, your body or what happens to you, you will be controlled. I'm not talking about predators or victims here (there are always people who will try to overpower you) but rather an awareness that the Spirit of God has given us back control, and that we're not slaves anymore.

Your past does not define your future. Your reputation does not define your responsibility. If you didn't make great choices in the past, you get to change your future now with your actions. You get to be responsible and free today. God is in the business of dishing out new mercies every morning. That's what you get to eat today in order to fuel the freedom you will walk in tomorrow. That's not to say that we must pretend none of that happened. On the contrary, the ability to see your past as God does is what empowers us to live in the future and in the present.

We can use our experiences to gain wisdom, and create a vision for our lives that extends past ourselves. Proverbs 29:18 says, "Where there is no prophetic vision the people cast off restraint, but blessed is he who keeps the law." When I decided to be pure as a young woman and to save myself for my husband, I knew that I wasn't living for the present, I was living for the future. I made an investment knowing that something, someone, was waiting for me.

Understand there is always a spiritual release whenever there is obedience to refrain. When we are able to deny ourselves instant gratification, we are able to receive the pearl of great price. That's not to say that virginity is a prize to be given or received; that's a misconception we've had in the church. Let me demystify this for you. My virginity is not given to my spouse; my virginity is given to God. I'm not buying his purity with my purity. I didn't have to marry a virgin, for that matter, because my purity was before God. It was for Him, not for my husband. Even after marriage, I'm still pure because it belongs to God. There is reward still coming my way because of it.

The pearl is the reward of eternal satisfaction we feel through living a life of purity. Your ability to be pure, to save your body, to give yourself to God fully, is rewarding because it honors God, and it celebrates how you've been created. It's an act of worship before God. Do you ever regret spending time in the presence of God? Never. We never regret giving time to God. Trust me. You won't regret giving Him all of you.

If you haven't already, you get to give your purity to God right now. The moment you make that decision, everything else is washed away. God does not count the past against you, nor does He remember it. Now you get to honor Him with your choices and your heart. The ability to commit and surrender to Him makes you very powerful. The more honest you are about your own weakness and your past, the more you surrender, the more He can come in and make it right.

POWER BELIEF #4

The fourth power belief is that **I am honorable.**

The Bible says that we are only able to treat others as well as we treat ourselves. If I love myself, then I'm going to love you better. I'm going to treat you the way I want to be treated. When I know my value, I will honor God with my body.[1] If I know that I'm fully loved, I will know that others are, too. 1 John 4:19 says that we love because He first loved us. This means that our ability to love, to honor, to serve, comes from knowing what God has done in us and for us.

Do you know Christians that are angry, hard to please, and judgmental? What would you say if I told you that they probably believe that God, their Father, is the same way? Most of the time, those people grew up with parents who modeled the behavior to them, and it influenced their understanding of God's character. Many of us believe that God is hard on us. As a result, we are hard on ourselves and then we treat people the same way. It's a pretty damaging cycle. What is happening on the inside is going to reflect what's happening on the outside, creating patterns of behavior all around us.

If this is you, we're going to help you get rid of some of those lies in Chapter 4. If you see this in the people around you, understand that you can't change them. You can't fix them. You're not Jesus. You can't reach into a person and choose a belief, an emotion or a value in order for them to change. The only person you are responsible for is yourself. Your ability to say, "I'm honorable because I am valuable," will allow you to take a step back and refrain from getting any value from your ability to fix or change people. It will allow you to honor others, value them. It will enable you to love at all times. It will also allow you to honor the process and journey of the people around you. We don't always know what God is doing, but we can trust that His plans for them are good.

What do I mean when I'm talking about knowing our value? Let me illustrate it for you. If you were walking down the street and found two pennies — one rusted and scuffed, the other bright and shiny — which one would hold more value? Even though they seem different on the outside, beneath the surface they have the exact same value. Why do they have the same value? They are each worth one cent. That never changes. This is how God sees us.

It doesn't matter if you're as pure as the day you came out of your mother's womb or if you've been around the block a few times, at the end of the day we all have the same unchangeable value. Whether you're on stage preaching to thousands or browsing YouTube in your bedroom, we all look the same to God because He sees us through the finished work of the cross. He sees us through the lens of redemption. We all hold the same value to Him. That's how significant you are. Your value doesn't change based on what you do, or how you live your life.

> YOUR ABILITY TO HAVE AUTHORITY AND INFLUENCE, LOVE PEOPLE, AND GAIN FAVOR, WILL DEPEND ON WHAT YOU BELIEVE ABOUT YOURSELF AND HOW YOU LIVE IT OUT

Now you might be wondering, why does it matter to do good things then? Why are we doing what we're doing? The reason for this is because even though we have the same value, we don't all have the same influence, effectiveness or anointing. Your ability to have authority and influence, love people, and gain favor, will depend on what you believe about yourself and how you live it out. Your ability to show people God's love makes you very effective, but no matter how effective you are, your value will never change. That's why you can go in and out of being effective without your value changing. We must be able to say, "I'm valuable. I'm chosen. I'm accepted all of the time." This is vital in order to be confident in ourselves and powerful within our lives.

POWER BELIEF #5

The fifth power belief is **I am significant**.

You play a vital role in God's story. You are significant simply because you exist. It says in the Bible that you were born in this generation on purpose, for such a time as this.

In Acts 13:36, it says that when David was done fulfilling what he was supposed to do in his generation, he died. Understand you're not here just because two people decided to have a good time one night. God knew when your mother was impregnated with you, and that you would be  born into the generation you belonged in. You being born is evidence that you possess something that this generation needs. Your very being, your gifting, your greatness, your personality, your calling, and your heart, exists for a reason. God created you to be here today. Your significance comes from Him alone. He loves you, accepts you, has chosen you, delights in you, celebrates you, and cherishes you — that's why you are significant.

When we take hold of these beliefs, we live fully illuminated lives. That's how we do the right things, marry the right person, and live healthy, free lives. We become full people. You see, no matter what the world tells you, two half people don't ever make a whole person. You're looking for someone to compliment you, not complete you. Two whole people make a full, healthy relationship. As you believe God, trust Him, believe that you are powerful, honorable and significant, you will become whole.

We need to embrace all of these beliefs, not just a few. If there's a part of you that doesn't believe or trust God but you function effectively, you may still feel powerful and significant. But without knowing that God is trustworthy, you may feel a need to control things or perform for love. At your core, you'll still wonder if He's going to show up for you and take care of you. What if you are powerful, significant and trust God but aren't honorable? You might step over people on your way to the top. This is why it's important to have every aspect of these ingrained in us.

Whether you're single, married, a parent or grandparent, you will need a fully illuminated life in every situation you face. If each of these power beliefs were light bulbs, we would want all of them lit up in order to be completely illuminated. When we are full of light and life, we will create marriages and families full of powerful people. This is the point of it all: to disciple nations. We want to be powerful, free and whole so that we can create community around us. We want a powerful family culture. We want a powerful moral culture. In order to have that, we must start with ourselves.

We are not going to build a successful Kingdom culture if there are cracks in our foundation. If our men are not honorable, they may treat others as lesser-than. If women believe that their significance comes from their sexuality — how sexy or attractive they are — then there will be brokenness in the foundation. Women would start using their

PEOPLE SHOULD LOOK AT US AND SEE JESUS

sexuality as a weapon as they try to find power and significance in their environment, instead of in the arms of true Love.

People should look at us and see Jesus. If we don't move in power and truth, no one is going to see God in us. How could they? You know you are living a fully illuminated life when people look at you and see God. When you get fully illuminated, you have a bright future. You begin to change or build your legacy; a generation is better off because of you. Because of people who live fully illuminated — like a city on a hill — the world changes. Our churches change, our schools change, and our culture begins to build on a stable foundation.

Five Power Beliefs can change everything. I want us to take some time to evaluate these beliefs. What do we believe and what don't we believe? Let's get our hearts in position and ask God to show us. Let's close our eyes for a minute and take some time to ask God what you believe about Him. Ask Him what you believe about yourself. There are some of you who just realized that you don't trust God. That's okay. Ask Him what you need to do in order to give up fear. Let Him show you what His best is for you.

If you don't feel powerful, let these words enter your heart as you make a declaration over yourself: I come against condemnation that keeps me from being able to hear truth. I'm saying no to fear and yes to love. This is a new seaso. This is a new awakening of wisdom in my life. I am pure, holy and set apart. I walk in the greatness of God's Holy Spirit, in power, love and self-control.

Allow Him to teach you what this looks like.

Some of you are called to teach the next generation, as mothers and fathers, about this illuminated life. They're not going to have what you had; they get a fresh start. They're going to have a hope they've never had. God is going to illuminate His presence in you in such a way that you'll be anointed to teach on these things. God will fill your mouth in surprising and supernatural ways with the words you need. You're going to change your family, your culture and your history.

⑦ YES? NO? MAYBE?

So, now that we've discussed our history with sexuality, some lies we often believe, and some important truths about who God is and who we are, we're ready to ask the question:

What does God have to say about sex?

Let's go back, one more time, to that infamous place — the Garden of Eden. In Genesis 2 we read:

> ❝*God commanded the man, "you can eat from any tree in the garden except from the tree of the knowledge of good and evil. Don't eat from it. The moment you eat from that tree, you're dead*❞ (MSG).

ADAM AND EVE HAD THE FREEDOM TO CHOOSE WHETHER THEY WOULD OBEY GOD OR NOT

I know what you're thinking: "That doesn't say anything about sex. It doesn't even say very much about me!" You're right, it doesn't. However, it does give us a glimpse into something very important. At the beginning of creation, God put a man and a woman in a garden and gave them both one specific attribute. It's called a free will. (I'm sure you're familiar with the term.) Adam and Eve had the freedom to choose whether they would obey God or not.

Various theologians believe differently on the subject, but I believe that God put two trees — the tree of life and the tree of the knowledge of good and evil — in the garden so that He could actually prove that we have a free will. If there was only one tree, there wouldn't be a choice. There wouldn't even be an opportunity to exercise free will. There wouldn't be anything to decide, and it would simply be, "God loved man and man loved Him and they lived happily ever after." Instead,

He gave them an option so that He could be chosen and decidedly loved. He didn't want it to be forced, manipulated or unfair. We were free to love Him from the beginning. He's not afraid of being rejected by us — He's comfortable taking the risk. When it came to choosing the right way, there was no fear in Him. We can learn from Genesis that choice is the foundation of our lives.

The basis of who you are lives in Whom you've chosen. When you chose to believe in Jesus, you took on righteousness. In that moment, you came alive to who you were created to be. Yes, God chose us from before the foundation of the world; even in the garden, He knew you. But none of that will change you until you choose to walk into His arms. And, because He know us so well, knows that it can take time for us to renew our minds, learn to trust, and practice good choices, He put some guardrails up to let us know when we could be about to walk off a cliff. We call it the protective "no."

Let's flip back to Genesis 1, shall we? Start in verse 27, where God is beaming over His children, Adam and Eve, blessing them with the "yes" He had over their lives:

> **"***Prosper! Reproduce! Fill the Earth! Take charge! Be responsible for fish in the sea and birds in the air, for every living thing that moves on the face of Earth. Adam, they'll need names; express your creative nature! Go ahead son, name them! Oh, and when you get hungry, help yourself to every sort of seed-bearing plant on Earth, and every kind of fruit-bearing tree, whatever grows out of the ground — it's yours!***"*

That's a lot of yes — yes, have a fulfilling, abundant life! Yes, have lots of sex! Yes, make lots of babies! Yes, be the boss and make the world what you want it to be. Yes, be creative! And my personal favorite — yes, eat whatever you want! Yes, enjoy everything I made!

Now, skip ahead to chapter 2, verse 16.

"Adam, there's just one thing I have to tell you — there's one tree that I don't want you to eat from. See that one in the middle of the garden? Yes, that one. Everything else is yours, except for that one. The fruit on that one tree is like poison— the moment you eat from that tree, you're dead!"

Sound familiar?

Now, I'm a mom of four boys. Most days, my life consists of wiping faces and changing diapers, picking up and stepping on Legos while listening to Elmo's World over a pile of laundry. My favorite words to hear are, "Yes, Mommy." My least favorite is, "No!" (And all the parents who've ever raised a toddler said, amen!)

Some days I feel like "no" is the only word I say. I'm sure that my boys feel the same: "No! Don't touch that, it's hot!" "No, you may not use your brother as a drum." "No, you may not eat sugar for breakfast, lunch and dinner." "No, the force won't make me forget about it; this is the homework I'm looking for." It can feel like my "no" is bigger than my "yes." Am I saying no because I take pleasure in withholding fun and adventure from my boys? Is it because I don't want them to be happy, or experience life to its fullest? Of course not. I say no because I want them to live to see adulthood. I say no to protect them.

When it comes to sex, God's only "no" is a protective no.

WHEN IT COMES TO SEX, GOD'S ONLY "NO" IS A PROTECTIVE NO

As your Father in Heaven, your Creator, and your Friend, He wants to see you live a full, happy, healthy life. There's not a lot that hurts more — or lingers longer — than pain from sexual baggage. It can come from many different experiences: abuse, losing your virginity to someone who never loved you, being dumped, hookups full of shame and regret, adultery, infidelity or even diseases that tear both bodies and families apart. He knows this, and so, in His deep concern for your well-being, He says:

"No! Stop! Wait! You're going to fall! You can't fly. You weren't made for this. You're not indestructible! This isn't going to be good for you!"

The only time God says 'no' to sex is when sex is not protected, or maybe I should say, when we are not protected. God never designed sex to be experienced a la carte. It is part of a package deal. You can't take an orgasm and leave the bonding. You can't take a crazy adventure and leave the memories. You can't take a one-night stand and leave your heart behind. The connection that takes place during sex is so profound and divine; it joins us body to body, soul to soul and spirit to spirit. It changes and touches us forever. Because of the way sex affects us and because of its God-given purpose, it must be covered within a commitment that says you're in it for life, in the context of family and community. Sex needs to be protected within covenant and marriage. We need it to be. (Skip ahead to Chapter 3 and 4 for more on that.)

> GOD NEVER DESIGNED SEX TO BE EXPERIENCED A LA CARTE. IT IS PART OF A PACKAGE DEAL

While many of us get stuck believing that God has a big "no" for everything, I think that more of us get stuck in a 'maybe' as we're trying to figure it out. Sitting on the fence, we get bitter, feeling like we're in a tug-of-war between our sex drive and the rules. If that's you today, I'd encourage you to begin to meditate on God's "yes" in place of His "no". When we embrace the truth that God actually has a big "yes" about many things, we begin to accept His "no" — His one, protective "no"— with much more hope and expectancy.

Begin to renew your mind to these truths:

God loves you and He knows your every desire. He made sex and said it was good. He says yes to healthy relationships. He says yes to romance. He says yes to friendships. He says yes to beautiful wives. He says yes to studly husbands. He says yes to babies. He says yes to families. He says yes to His children growing to full maturity and experiencing abundant life. No more maybes.

⑧ SAFETY FIRST

So, let's go back to Adam and Eve for a moment. God gave them the information they needed to thrive in the garden, so what did they need to do? All they needed to do was live with boundaries. A powerful person understands that they possess power and knowledge, and with that comes the responsibility to employ boundaries to protect themselves.

Throughout our society, we see the same need for protection. We have rules, laws, and boundaries to safeguard society. Take traffic laws for example. How many times do you want people to follow these laws? 80% of the time? How about 90%? It's safe to say that we all want them to be enforced and followed 100% of the time. (Except, of course, when we're personally caught speeding.) We want people to stop at red lights and use turn signals. Why? Because it regulates safety and keeps us aware of the people around us.

This is the same when it comes to our bodies and our sexuality. What's in place to protect you? Who do you hang out with? What do you wear? What kinds of movies do you watch? Who do you let touch you, and how? You make hundreds of decisions every day that either endanger or protect you. While your mind processes these choices, there is a gate they have to pass through to be acted upon. Who is this gatekeeper? Your will. And you must learn to control it.

For example, our will and our desires are quite powerfully interconnected. Many of us know that when we want something, we will do anything to get it. If you think, I want ice cream tonight, you will get ice cream even if you have to sell a limb to get it. (Or is that just me?) Regardless, if we think of something, we'll make it happen. Our thoughts and desires have incredible strength. Where our brain goes, our body goes. Scientifically and statistically, our decisions are already prepared in our brain before we even do anything.[2]

Sometimes, our desires feel so strong that it's hard to say no. This is where you get to decide if your desires make your decisions, or if you do. This is the time to put your will to work; you get to learn to tell yourself what to do! You get to put up boundaries for yourself — where you'll go or not go, when you'll go to bed, what you'll eat or drink — and then do it. You are not victim to your own choices.

When it comes to making good choices and saying "yes" to the right things, we need to recognize that we possess a lot of power, and our sexuality holds a lot of power. As men and women, our emotions, ways of processing information, communication styles, desires and motivators all play powerful roles in our lives. We must understand this about ourselves if we want to be powerful people who make powerful decisions. We need to see the full picture of who we are, including the power of our sexuality, if we are going to live lives full of wisdom and understanding.

WE NEED TO SEE THE FULL PICTURE OF WHO WE ARE, IF WE ARE GOING TO LIVE LIVES FULL OF WISDOM AND UNDERSTANDING.

03 SEX And THE BODY

To love at all is to be vulnerable.

C.S. LEWIS, THE FOUR LOVES

⑨ THE TWILIGHT ZONE

Calloused hands parted the linen curtains as he strolled out onto the balcony; each step strong and sure. His bronze arms flexed as they took the weight of his body, leaning over the guardrail. The spring heat danced off the rooftops, giving the illusion of waves; doves rode them as they took to their roosts for the evening. Drawing a steady breath, his bright eyes studied the horizon, deliberately, as though he had lost something. His handsome face creased with unease.

It was springtime, the season when most kings took their soldiers out to fight, as was his custom. He had been a man of war his whole life. He was built for it, designed for it. He was a fine soldier, having honed his skills since his youth. He could do wonders with only five stones. Lions, bears and even giants were no match for him. He had slain thousands — no, tens of thousands — of enemies. He was loved by the people. No, favor had not always been his, but anointing — he certainly had anointing. And as long as he remained faithful, well, God had never let him down before.

That fateful evening he found no rest in his bedchambers. His men away at war, and he, at home in the palace? His soul wrestled, unable to find peace. The sun had not quite set, so David roused himself and took to the roof for some fresh air. As he strolled along, something glistened in the corner of his vision. A reflection on water.

From his vantage point he could see her clearly: a woman bathing on a roof below his. She was stunningly beautiful. Bathsheba, the wife of one of his finest officers. If looks could kill, well, he would already be dead. Unable to shake her from his mind, he gave in to his passion. Vulnerable and without comfort, the king called her to join him in his palace....

Pause.

Now, if you've been in church for any amount of time, you probably know how the story goes from here:

David and Bathsheba have a little rendezvous in the royal bedchambers. After having sex (and you thought I wasn't going to say it), David sends her home. Before long, she realizes she is pregnant with David's child. David knows that there's no way he can pass the baby off as Uriah's, since Bathsheba had just finished her period and her husband is at the battlefront. So, he tries to get Uriah to come home and make love to her. The plan fails. David kills Uriah to cover up his mess. (See 1 Samuel 11 for the full story.)

Here's the question:

What happened to David? What went so wrong with this great hero, anointed king and man after God's own heart, that he became an adulterer, liar and coward? I would like to suggest to you that the same thing happened to him that happens to many of us: he chose to behave in such a way that violated his God-given design.

You see, David was called by God to be a warrior in his generation. He was anointed to rule and to take back territory for God, to build the nation of Israel. When he walked in this identity and followed the "yes" God had over his life, he was virtually indestructible. But when David chose to not embrace his calling to go to war, he violated the way he was made. He denied himself what he was made for. He became open and vulnerable, and it was all too easy for him to fill the void with something, or in his case someone, who didn't belong there.

Believe it or not, the same story is repeating itself in hundreds of lives, all over the world, right now. No, we're not all strolling the rooftops at sunset, scouting out our next baby-mama; but many of us are failing to embrace God's design and calling in our lives when it comes to our sexuality.

Why?

Well, maybe it's because we never understood our design in the first place.

⑩ SPIRIT AND SOUL AND BODY, OH MY!

If you did not grow up in the church, you may never have been told that you are more than your physical body and your soul (your mind, will, and emotions). In the Bible there are two distinct meanings for the word soul. One is used to describe the life of the inner man, everything that makes up your personality. This includes your mind, your will, and your emotions. The other word, however, is the part that you may not know about. It describes that which makes a human body alive.[1] This is the "soul" that departs from a dying person, or that is given back in order that a dead person might live. We would call this your spirit. The Bible talks about all three parts in 1 Thessalonians 5:23:

"Now may the God of peace Himself sanctify you entirely; and may your spirit and soul and body be preserved complete, without blame at the coming of our Lord Jesus Christ."

The Bible explains that we are triune beings — body, soul, and spirit. We can think of ourselves like an archery target or dartboard. On the inside — the bulls eye — we have a spirit, on the next circle is our soul, and on the outside is our body.

THE BIBLE EXPLAINS THAT WE ARE TRIUNE BEINGS – BODY, SOUL, AND SPIRIT.

They all need to be preserved, they all need to be respected, and they all need to be understood. Each is part of the whole. They have different functions that lend themselves to the full body. If one part of the body isn't functioning, the others cannot properly move forward either. When I have a migraine, I simply cannot function to my full capacity. If you have a broken foot, good luck moving around quickly. All three parts have desires, needs and appetites that are real and need to be satisfied in a healthy way. (Skip to Chapter 5 for more about that.)

When it comes to our sexuality, we get into trouble when we either don't understand what these three parts are doing, or when we try to separate them from each other. This is what media communicates to us: Sex is just a physical encounter. Why are you getting so emotional about it? Why do you feel guilty? You're both old enough to make that decision. It's all good! Here's the problem: you can't engage one part of yourself without it affecting the others. You can't build up your spirit-man without it changing your soul and body. Your thoughts, feelings, and desires always show themselves through your physical actions. You can't use your body without your emotions being involved. You weren't designed that way.

Even while we're being told that sex is a one-dimensional experience, most of our culture can communicate that there is more to it than we realize. At one time or another we have all experienced feelings of attachment, jealousy or loyalty toward someone, even though we may not have had the words to describe it. It's safe to say that most of the time, we're not great at defining love or what sex really consists of. Something deeper is happening, but no one can quite put their finger on it. There's more to it than meets the eye.

If you don't know what I'm talking about, simply listen to the top hundred love songs of all time. Love hurts, love completes us. It lifts us up, it tears us apart. It's instant, it's insatiable. We need it, we want it, we can't get enough of it. It's powerful, it's forever, near and far, always together. We're crazy in love. We're hopelessly devoted.

Without an explanation as to what is going on inside of us, we are left to be tossed to and fro by intense feelings, emotional roller coasters, and physical impulses. It can make it difficult to make healthy choices in line with the way God made us — body, soul, and spirit. When we are educated and informed in a holistic way, we are prone to make better choices. We need to understand how it all fits together as a multi-dimensional experience.

> **ALL OF US HAVE A PART INSIDE OF US THAT IS PREPARED TO HOLD THE SPIRIT OF GOD, WHETHER WE KNOW IT OR NOT.**

Let's start by talking about the spirit.

Everyone has a spirit. All of us have a part inside of us that is prepared to hold the Spirit of God, whether we know it or not. We were made by God and for God. He designed us with the capacity to be eternally united with Him. Your spirit, the Bible says, was dead until you invited the Holy Spirit to come and live inside of you.

Before the Holy Spirit came to live inside of you, your spirit was like a deflated balloon. But when you made the choice to accept Jesus as your Lord and Savior, inviting His Spirit to come live inside of you, it was like that balloon inflated. Your spirit came alive, and for the first time you began to live.

How many of us remember this moment in our own life? The world looked different; colors became brighter, everything felt new. Nothing changed, yet everything changed. You began to hear God's voice. You began to want to do what's right. You became awake to the reality of how you were created. The Bible says you got a new heart and new desires. From that moment on you were able to be led by your spirit man, under the direction of the Holy Spirit.

John 16:13 says the Spirit leads us, through our human spirit, into all truth and convicts us of what's not right. One of the main job descriptions of the Holy Spirit is to convict us of sin. He's not condemning us. There's a big difference between condemnation and conviction. Conviction allows us to know what we're doing and to change. Conviction, in fact, empowers us to change. Condemnation says, "You don't have any power to change. What's wrong with you? Hide it." Conviction may make you feel overwhelmed by the knowledge of the wrong done, but it will always lead you into what is right.

Your spirit, if you are born again, is involved in every decision you make and every action you take. Or, at least, it should be. We can do our best to ignore our spirit when the Holy Spirit is talking to us, but when we do, we can grieve Him. We will experience guilt and shame and a sense of separation from God. When it comes to our sexuality, it is vital to understand that you cannot separate your spirit from your soul or body. Whatever you do affects you spiritually. It affects your relationship with God. Our spirit exists to keep us connected to God, not only for eternal relationship with Him, but to help us live abundant, healthy lives now. This is why Paul teaches us to, "walk in the Spirit, and let the Spirit bring order to [our lives]. If [we] do, [we] will never give in to [our] selfish and sinful cravings" (Galatians 5:16, The VOICE).

Let's look at the soul next.

We know that we have a soul because we experience it. Your soul holds three specific things. It holds your mind, will, and emotions. Your thoughts come from your mind. Your feelings come from your emotions Your determination and decisions come from your will. All three of these are our responsibility to renew. The Bible doesn't say that we renew our spirit, it says that we renew our soul.

We know that our spirit is alive in Christ and it already knows what's right. So, if we walk according to the Holy Spirit, and we want to do what's right, why do we do what's wrong? If we have a new heart and new desires, what's happening? To start with, understand that this is a common issue. Paul wrote about it in Romans 7:15: "For I do not understand my own actions. For I do not do what I want, but I do the very thing I hate." We can all relate with this, can't we?

Why is this the case? Well, the simple explanation is that your soul has been with you for a long time. We can't get rid of mister soul, but we can, over time, change his ways by aligning ourselves with God's Spirit in a renewal process. Yes, that's our responsibility, but He will help us through the process. The key word here is process. It's not going to happen right away. It's going to take some time.

Now, you may be wondering: with the Spirit of God living in our spirit, don't we have a new identity? Aren't we defined by Christ in us? Does this mean that we are supposed to become cookie-cutter-Christians, all looking, thinking, and acting just like Jesus? Yes, and no.

WHEN WE CAME TO JESUS, WE DIDN'T LOSE OUR SOULS, WE GAINED HIS SPIRIT.

When we came to Jesus, we didn't lose our souls, we gained His Spirit. Our soul is our personality; it holds everything that makes us unique. God loves diversity. If He wanted everyone to be the same, He would have made us that way in the first place. This means that our personality isn't going die away, but we are to become transformed in our sense of identity and character until we are like Him.

The soul is the mental and emotional component of our sexuality. It is what makes us male and female on the inside. It is the seat of our desires, our memories, our pain, and our pleasure. Try as we may to separate our soul from our physical actions, it is impossible. God designed us in such a way that our body, mind, will, and emotions would work together to create a complete sexual expression. With all these parts working in harmony, being led by the Spirit, we are able us to experience the euphoria and deep satisfaction that God always intended for us. If we try to have one without the other, we are withholding from ourselves the very thing for which we were designed. (More about that a little later.)

Lastly, but not least: the body.

Our body is, very simply, our flesh and bones. It includes our organs, our brain, our physiological systems, nerves, muscles, tissues, etc. They all work together to keep us alive. Our body contains our spirit and soul. It also is the home of a wonderful thing called your sex drive.

⑪ KICKING INTO OVERDRIVE

In Chapter 2, we explored that God has a 'yes' when it comes to sex. In the garden, Adam and Eve were put there for partnership, intimacy and connection — and yes, to have sex. It's fair to say that sex wasn't a big surprise to God. He didn't stumble upon them moving around in some bushes and say, "Oh my goodness! What's going on here? Angels close your eyes!" He knew exactly what they were doing. He created them to fit together, to be together, and to be connected. They would fit together both physically and spiritually. He gave them a desire for companionship, and in order to seek this partnership, He gave them a sex drive. He gave you and me the same thing.

> HE GAVE IT TO US SO THAT WE WOULD LEARN TO STEWARD AND MANAGE SOMETHING POWERFUL, VALUABLE, AND SIGNIFICANT

Have you ever wondered why He gives us a sex drive long before we are married and can have sex? Wouldn't it have been easier to just give it to us on our wedding night? Did He give it to us just to torture us? He gave it to us so that we would learn to steward and manage something powerful, valuable, and significant.

What exactly is a sex drive, you ask? It's a complicated answer but let's try our best to define it. Having a sex drive means:

You want to have sex with someone.

I know, it's profound. If you're underlining things, you'll want to carefully highlight that sentence. (I kid.)

So, God gave us a desire to have sex with people. Brilliant. The question now is, why? Why give us a burning desire to unite ourselves with another human being? To start this section off, I want us to understand why God made us this way. I like to say that there are three B's that explain why we have a sex drive.

The first B, if you will, is to make **babies**.

When you have sex, you can make a baby. How do I know that? Many hours of research. Actually, I happen to have four babies, so I know a thing or two about it.

God gave us a sex drive so that we would want to procreate. There are many things that could prevent us from choosing to have babies — financial security, career, independence, wanting a full night's sleep — but when it comes down to it, we were meant to have children. This was God's command for us: be fruitful and multiply. He designed us in such a way that it would be natural for us to do it. He enjoys giving children to families as a blessing, and as a way of redemption. We see this throughout scripture with the stories of Abraham and Isaac, Hagar and Ishmael, and Hannah and Samuel, just to name a few. He gave babies to barren couples who had no possible way to conceive. The Savior of the world even came through a blessing that God bestowed on Mary when He miraculously put life into her womb. What an honor for her to carry Jesus and raise Him in our world. The greatest blessings come in small packages: babies.

> THE SAVIOR OF THE WORLD EVEN CAME THROUGH A BLESSING THAT GOD BESTOWED ON MARY WHEN HE MIRACULOUSLY PUT LIFE INTO HER WOMB.

I know some of you may be thinking: but not everyone can have babies, what about those that can't? Just because someone has a situation where they're not able to have babies, doesn't mean that the entire human race was not created to have babies.

Let me give you an example: I had an emergency cesarean. Surgery saved our first son's life. But it would be ridiculous for me to conclude that women were only made to have C-sections since that's what happened to me. Just because my anatomy did not work properly doesn't allow me to write off the way the female anatomy of the human race operates. My experience does not negate the entire human experience.

It is an undeniable fact that God made women to have babies. He gave women wombs. He did not give men wombs. He did not give men fallopian tubes, nor he did not give them vaginas. He did not give them breasts or milk to feed the babies. He gave women bodies to nourish and birth babies. Our whole makeup and physical anatomy give us obvious signs that our entire design is to give birth to babies.

We know that this reality is both the beauty and danger of sexual intercourse. When we have sex outside of marriage, a child doesn't have the guaranteed security that it would have within covenant. When a married husband and wife have sex, the baby is born in the context of (hopefully) healthy partnership and commitment. God also wants a baby to be born with a feminine and masculine counterpart. This is why it is important that a man and woman parent a child together.

If a child does not have a mother or a father, it is critical that they find masculine or feminine relationships to cultivate the masculine or feminine heart in them. This is God's perfect plan for families and community. I understand that many of us come from single parent homes, divorced families, foster care, or other less than ideal circumstances; but we must understand what God's intention was and aim for that. It doesn't mean that God won't redeem something less than ideal. It simply means that we can aim for something higher in order to teach culture about what is best for us.

Without a sex drive, we would be deterred from choosing a partner, bonding with them for life, and having children. The connection, intimacy, and pleasure we are rewarded with when we listen to our sex drive are important and highly motivational. Without them, we might not have a desire to even be in relationship with people, let alone procreate with them.

The second B is **beauty**.

In the book of Proverbs, Solomon, the wisest person in history says: "There are three things that are too amazing for me, four that I do not understand: the way of an eagle in the sky, the way of a snake on a rock, the way of a ship on the high seas, and the way of a man with a young woman."2 To him, there was something inexplicably beautiful that occurred between the two.

> **WITHOUT A SEX DRIVE, WE WOULD BE DETERRED FROM CHOOSING A PARTNER, BONDING WITH THEM FOR LIFE, AND HAVING CHILDREN.**

Here's the deal: The devil did not create sex. In case you missed the last few chapters, let's just get that out there. Justin Timberlake is not bringing sexy back. God created sex. God is the sexiest being alive. He knows what's sexy. He knows how we were made, and He knows what we need to have. He knows what looks right, what feels right, and how we are to experience sex without shame, condemnation, naivety, or pain. He created all of this for us as a beautiful thing to explore. You've probably heard, "The devil can't create anything new, he can only pervert it." He's been trying for a long time to redefine sex, twist and recreate it, but no one else can define sex for us the way that God has.

What the devil can't recreate is what happens when a man and woman have a sexual encounter in covenant. He cannot create beauty. He cannot create wonder, mystery or glory. He can try to diminish it, lie to you, and say it's not a big deal. He can try to get you to connect with a bunch of people and become desensitized to it. What he cannot do is recreate the beauty of what happens when two bodies come together.

The intimacy of two becoming one cannot be counterfeited. He will always try to bring a counterfeit, but there's a real sexual encounter that God intended for you to have. It's meant to be fulfilling, healthy and happy, and part of who He is. It's supposed to be glorious!

> **THE INTIMACY OF TWO BECOMING ONE CANNOT BE COUNTERFEITED.**

Having a desire and a yearning for another — our spouse, in particular — is a beautiful thing. Being together in extreme intimacy and ultimate pleasure is beautiful. I believe that for God, there's nothing more beautiful than this.

The third B is **bonding**.

Matthew 19:4–6 says:

> *"Haven't you read in your Bible that the Creator originally made man and woman for each other, male and female? And because of this, a man leaves his father and mother and is firmly bonded to his wife, becoming one flesh — no longer two bodies but one. Because God created this organic union of the two sexes, no one should desecrate His art by cutting them apart"* (MSG).

Our sex drive allows us to connect with our spouse and create a bond for life. It's the glue that seals us together. As much as we'd like to think we're rubber and people can just bounce off of us, the reality is that when we have sexual encounters, we're being glued together. There's a bonding that occurs that supersedes a mere skin-to-skin connection. Scientifically, we know that it engages us hormonally, neurologically, psychologically; it forms intense bonds mentally, emotionally, and physically, especially when we do it over and over again.[3] (We'll explore this thoroughly in the next section.)

WHETHER WE KNOW IT OR NOT, SEX TOUCHES OUR WHOLE BEING.

Whether we know it or not, sex touches our whole being. Many of us already know this because we've experienced how we become deeply attached to the people we're intimate with. You might not even like someone that you've been involved with, but you feel as though you love them. You feel like you can't live without them. It's because of the intimacy, history and connection you've shared. It's like we become addicted to them. Did you know that this was God's plan from the start? God designed us this way so that we would be faithful, committed, and loyal to our spouse in a way that defies will and emotion.

⑫ YOUR BIGGEST SEX ORGAN

It is time! Now that we have gained an understanding of God, our identity, our power, our choices, and a little about how we are made, we're ready to talk about it. Let's talk about sex! It's time to take a look at what's going on in our bodies on a biological level. I hope that the scientific details I'm about to share will help see that all of this isn't just based in theological opinion, but is rooted in our biological design as human beings.

Let's first define sex. You'd think this would be pretty clear, but I've found that this isn't always the case. Sex is intercourse between two people, right? This includes anything that has the word sex in it (vaginal sex, anal sex, oral sex). This is true according to the Bible, as well as science. This also extends to cover sexual experiences that did not include some kind of penetration. Any behavior that causes arousal and sexual stimulation falls under the category of sex.

Follow me for a minute — I know some of you are thinking, How can this be true? Are you saying that because I've made out with my girlfriend or boyfriend, we've had sex? No, not exactly, but at the same time, yes.

Here's the deal: the human brain registers any sexual activity as sex.[4] Scientific research tells us that all sexual activity will affect us on a chemical and emotional level, regardless of whether it goes all the way to intercourse. Masturbation? Sex. Oral? Sex. Yes, you read that correctly. Whether it's masturbation, having intercourse, or experiencing an orgasm through oral stimulation, the brain receives the same information. It interprets the stimulation in the same way it would with sex. Consequently, you experience the same effects, physically and emotionally. This is why it can be just as satisfying to have an orgasm by yourself as it is with a partner. This is why you feel so attached to someone you only made out with.

> SCIENTIFIC RESEARCH TELLS US THAT ALL SEXUAL ACTIVITY WILL AFFECT US ON A CHEMICAL AND EMOTIONAL LEVEL

When your brain responds and releases its reward and pleasure hormones, you get the "high". It doesn't matter what particular behavior you were enjoying at the time because to your brain it's all the same. "But, we didn't have intercourse. We just did oral. That means we're still pure because we didn't have sex, right?" Looks like some of us are in for a rude awakening.

There are three specific hormones (chemical-messengers of the body that communicate with one another and complete various processes) that we're going to discuss as we venture to understand our bodies: endorphins, oxytocin and vasopressin. When these particular hormones are released, they cause us to bond to the activities, individuals and objects that gave us pleasure. This explains why our thoughts can be overtaken by previous encounters. This is why we never forget the people we have sex with. How does this happen? I'm glad you asked.

Let's start with our endorphins: dopamine and serotonin. I like to call these our "happy" chemicals. These chemicals cause an intense rush of pleasure and increase our ability to focus and concentrate. Dopamine is also known as "the reward hormone". When we do something that excites us, this little guy comes into the brain cells to confirm a feeling of excitement.[5] What happens when we feel this reward? We seek it again. It's the same as when we reward children for using the potty — they will do it again for no other reason than to get the reward. Dopamine is necessary for basic functioning because it gives us the necessary boldness required to take risks. It helps us motivate ourselves to do everyday things like get out of bed in the morning.

> GOD DESIGNED YOU TO HAVE THIS REWARD CHEMICAL SO THAT WHEN YOU'RE MARRIED YOU TWO WOULD CONNECT DEEPLY

It's important that we understand this: when we have a sexual encounter, the chemical release in our brain allows us to feel rewarded, and causes the desire to do it over and over again. This may be the reason why many of us are caught up in addictions, struggling to abstain, or find it challenging to move on from past encounters. Inside, a very basic, fundamental and God-given part of us is just seeking a reward.

God designed you to have this reward chemical so that when you're married and you begin to have sex with your spouse, you two would connect deeply, not only on your honeymoon night, but over and over again. This would cause you to stay joined, bonded, as one-flesh, united for your whole life together. That kind of intimacy was intended to be shared with one person only. God wants you to bond with your spouse in such a way that when you go into the bedroom, you feel rewarded, and desire to repeatedly return to that person. And it all happens because of the little chemicals we call endorphins.

Another chemical at play in the brain is oxytocin. This is a trust and pair-bonding hormone. While both genders have this hormone, oxytocin primarily functions in the female brain. It can be released by a number of different activities.[6] Not all of these activities are sexual.

Oxytocin allows a woman to bond to the most significant people in her life. It eases stress, creating feelings of calm and closeness, which leads to increased trust. One of the most significant bonds for a woman is the one between herself and her baby. The oxytocin that gets released in a woman's body during breastfeeding or close contact allows her to bond to that child unlike any other, alerting her brain to nurture and protect it.

Moms, could you imagine if you felt responsible for every baby you saw like it was your very own? Mothers everywhere would be yelling, "It's my baby! No, it's my baby! Give him to me, he's mine!" It would become a real issue for everyone, everywhere. But this just isn't the case. We weren't built that way.

If you've ever had a baby, you know this to be true: as a mother, you bond to your baby like no other child in the world. It is a feeling and attachment you simply can't explain. It is an incredibly valuable connection. We need the instinct that says, "You touch my baby and I will cut you." Okay, maybe not quite that aggressive, but something that says, "This is my baby and I'll take care of it, no matter what." God created something to be released inside of a woman that attaches her to child and husband. It protects the covenant, the family, and the connection.

WHETHER IT'S A ONE-TIME ENCOUNTER OR A LIFELONG COMMITMENT, WE BOND THE SAME WAY.

What makes things even more interesting is that these hormones are values-neutral.[7] Whether it's a one-time encounter or a lifelong commitment, we bond the same way. It also crystallizes these emotional memories in our minds, making these encounters and experiences difficult to forget. As much as we believe in God's power over us to help redeem memories, it was not His intention to clean things up for us repeatedly. Again, if it's our responsibility to renew our minds, we make things more difficult for ourselves when our lifestyle doesn't match our vision for wholeness. When you are together with your spouse in marriage, the idea is that you would feel safe and calm with them, without the past interfering with your connection.

As you can see, there are obvious reasons why we're all messed up as a society. We say that intimate encounters don't mean anything; our biological design says differently. We shouldn't be surprised when we, as women, can't quite get over a "casual" encounter. You know what it looks like when this happens: we still pick up the phone when they call, we take care of them when they're sick, we put our trust in them when they aren't trustworthy. When we do these things, all we're doing is reinforcing a bond, making it more difficult to separate ourselves from that individual when we need to. A powerful part of us still wants to nurture that someone who hasn't made a commitment to us. Why? Because we were designed to bond to a person beyond our will and emotions.

God, in His infinite wisdom, knew that some days marriage would get hard. He knew we would need some help choosing each other day after day, over and over again. He knew that some days we wouldn't like our spouse very much. We would argue. Bills would come in. Babies would get sick. In-laws would come to town. Emergencies would happen. Stress would overshadow the relationship. So, He installed an override system (hormones) that would cause us to stick together through thick and thin, in good times and bad, for richer or for poorer, in sickness and in health. It would cause us to feel devoted, loyal, possessive, and willing to endure trials to keep what belongs to us. What an intelligent Designer we have.

The last hormone I want to talk about is vasopressin. Vasopressin is very similar to oxytocin, except that it is primarily released in the brain of men. This hormone causes a man to bond to a woman during intimate contact. I like to call it the "commitment hormone" or "monogamy molecule". This hormone generates a desire for commitment and rouses loyalty. It inspires a protective sense over one's mate, and can create a "jealous" tendency.[8]

While vasopressin is a highly valuable hormone, this chemical causes some problems when a relationship doesn't last. We often see this with the "jealous ex". You know the story: The captain of the football team with his big muscles and charming smile pursues the head cheerleader. A few magical dates later, he has fallen for her. She became his world — vasopressin got the better of him. Now she's gone, and he still feels bitterly connected to her. It's like she belongs to him. Nothing will be right until she is back on his arm. He begins to use manipulation and control to keep her close. First, nice gestures. When she declines, he moves onto guilt. Then rumors. Then bullies anyone who shows an interest in her. Okay, maybe that's a bit dramatic, but you get the picture. It can get ugly.

VASOPRESSIN ALSO DRIVES A MAN TO PROTECT HIS TERRITORY AND OFFSPRING, HEIGHTENING HIS SENSE OF RESPONSIBILITY.

Vasopressin also drives a man to protect his territory and offspring, heightening his sense of responsibility. Generally, this will happen with both genders, but men in particular will suddenly feel very responsible for a woman. We may think, calm down, Romeo! You're not even married! She's not even your wife! But in reality, he has had this hormone released in him and it tells him that he must protect her.

God knew what He was doing when He was programming our bodies, as men and women. He created us in such a way that we would instinctively fill roles within a male-female relationship. Our hormones cause us to do this. In a healthy relationship, they lead a man to forsake all others for his wife, and to put his children before himself. They encourage a woman to want only her husband, and to keep her children close. Our hormones are a beautiful gift meant to inspire a lifelong attachment, ensuring the success of a marriage and family.

IN SHORT, WOMEN HAVE A HORMONE THAT ENSURES THEY ARE NURTURING, WHILE MEN HAVE A HORMONE THAT ENSURES THEY PROTECT AND PRESERVE.

In short, women have a hormone that ensures they are nurturing, while men have a hormone that ensures they protect and preserve. We were both designed to seek each other repetitively for sexual intimacy and pleasure. Seems like a good combination, doesn't it? God designed men and women in such a way that we are perfectly complementary according to our calling and design. Women were created with the ability to bring children into this world; to nurture and comfort. Men were created with an innate ability to serve and protect; to provide and help raise their families.

This doesn't mean that if you're a woman you need to be a Suzy homemaker, baking cookies at home all the time. Nor does it mean that if you're a man that you're the policeman of your home. However, it does mean there are appropriate characteristics that belong to both genders. We don't want women who aren't nurturing having children because it's not a safe place for them. We want that aspect to be present and embraced. Similarly, we don't want men to leave their families unprotected. We want men to be loyal to their wives, their children, and create a safe place for them.

It's possible that many of us have felt foolish, powerless, or incompetent because of ways we've acted in the past. Any shame that has latched on as a result of past encounters or experiences needs to go. Being aware of how you've been created is the first step to understand that there's nothing wrong with you. We all need Christ to strengthen us. You'll need to partner with Him to renew your mind in order to break some patterns in your life. Begin to embrace God's design for your sexuality; understand it, respect it and value it. It takes time to change, but nothing is impossible.

⑬ WHEN TWO BECOME ONE

Wow. I'm impressed! You made it through the science lesson (or maybe you skipped over it after you read endorphins and met me here. No shame. Nice to have you back!). At this point, I'd like to zoom out and discuss what all this bonding looks like and how it affects us on a really practical level.

An illustration I like to use is this:

You could say that all of us are like a piece of tape with a certain amount of stickiness. We are born this way. Our stickiness is meant to bond us to another person. When we do everything right with one person, we are connected for life.

Our brains create new pathways that are strengthened by the continuous bonding with another. But, when we connect with people and then separate, it feels like a tearing has occurred.

When we don't realize this aspect of how we're designed, we end up torn in many ways — body, soul, and spirit. Separating from people is painful. Why? Because we're designed in such a way that it should be painful. We shouldn't want to leave someone so quickly. We should be inspired by loyalty, nurturing the other person and committing to them. It should be difficult for a husband to leave his wife, or for a mother to leave her family. You've invested your heart, your body, your time, and your emotions. You've shared pieces of you that you can't get back. This is the reason why we can't stay fully whole and fully intact when we rip away.

What happens in our society when we disregard how we're designed? We expect to go from relationship to relationship, sexual encounter to sexual encounter, like nothing is affecting us. That might not be you, but that's how a great percentage of the world functions. Most of the time, we're not required to make a commitment to anyone in order to get what we want. But the reality is that we sacrifice being whole and pain-free for convenient, selfish living.

What happens is this: when we have repeated sexual encounters, we lose our stickiness. Scientifically, we know this.[9] As we bond and break, bond and break, bond and break, we lose our ability to properly bond. When we're ready for that new, serious relationship or marriage, something is missing that prevents us from fully bonding; we don't feel that connected or committed. Our feelings may seem to diminish. When we see someone else a little more exciting, more appealing, more perfect for us, we're ready to move on in a heartbeat. The condition of being "crazy in love" suddenly disappears. We may say we don't feel all that excited anymore. We may even lose faith in falling in love again. Why is this happening?

One reason is that we have a generation that is taught to practice divorce. It tells us that if we're not getting what we need or what we want, we don't need to stick around. Connect as long as it feels good. Try out different things before you seal the deal. Test drive the car before you buy it. After all, you can't pick your favorite restaurant before you've tried the others, right?

The church isn't any better when it comes to this. Statistically, the church's divorce rates are the same as everyone else.[10] People wonder what the problem is, but all along, psychologically and emotionally, they've been making and breaking connections with people throughout their life. Whether it was dating everyone in their youth group or partying hard at college, their past prevented them from feeling fully connected. Eventually, when they got together with the one they wanted to marry, they wondered why it didn't feel magical or special. Their stickiness had left them. This is why it is important to protect our purity; spirit, soul, and body.

We must understand that ability to be pure and save ourselves is not just physical. It's not just about giving your v-card to someone. That's not the point. The point is to keep our stickiness intact so that when God brings the right person, we connect with them for life.

> THE POINT IS TO KEEP OUR STICKINESS INTACT SO THAT WHEN GOD BRINGS THE RIGHT PERSON, WE CONNECT WITH THEM FOR LIFE.

If you don't feel that you have any stickiness right now, it's time to pull away from romantic relationships and abstain from sexual activity. Get before God and ask Him to help restore you to your original stickiness. You may not use these exact words, but simply ask for your ability to connect again. Go ahead and take some time now to do that. Begin to allow Him to realign you on the inside and outside, so that when He brings the right person, you'll be able to connect in such way that it divinely unites you for life.

⑭ REAL TALK

People bond to people. This is not just a Christian idea, but a scientific one. We already discussed the aspects of this when it comes to our brain and our relationships. But let's get real for a minute. Do you think you only bond to the people who stimulate you and those you have intimacy with? Think again.

How about when it comes to what we're looking at? Did you know that if you're looking at pornography, you're bonding to these individuals and visual experiences? The Bible says that we shouldn't even think about people with lust, let alone look at what people are doing in secret. Not only are we watching these things, but when we pleasure ourselves to something, we bond to that very thing. This is especially true when we experience an orgasm because the brain is being flooded with hormones that tell you to do it again, whatever it is.

As we do it again (and again), we begin to build a dependency on that activity for pleasure because (as we examined in the brain section) the chemicals released are values-neutral. They cannot differentiate between sexual activities that are healthy and those that are unhealthy when it comes time to build a bond. When you bond to something, you have no stickiness available to bond to someone else. The point? If you have formed a bond with pornography, the consequence may be an inability to connect or bond with a real person in front of you. Even Hugh Hefner, the founder of Playboy's multi-billion dollar porn industry, having access to the most desirable and sought after women, must have pornographic material in the bedroom for him to reach any climax.[11] I think its safe to say, his brain has been so bonded with hyper-performed sexualized images that a real flesh and blood person is not enough. It's a very dangerous reality.

What happens if we believe that we, or others, will be able to perform at the same level as those in the videos? Unrealistic expectations and ideals settle in as we think about all of the things they're going to do for us (and to us). In effect, we ruin our potential for happiness with a real person (some really need to hear that they're not marrying a sex slave — they're marrying a person. A person with real needs, emotions and desires). As we look at pornographic material, we may tell ourselves that they're only actors or models, but our hormones don't know that. We can bond internally to specific images, ideas, and fantasies to the point where "normal" sex with our spouse isn't exciting anymore. In a moment of weakness, we trade in our ability to bond to a real person for a fleeting moment with a performance. When we do this, we rob ourselves of the true intimacy, connection, and comfort that we need.

One last thing: It may shock you to learn that your spouse (most likely) won't want to have sex all of the time. No matter how hot you are. This prefaces our next topic, which will explain why self-control is not just something singles practice, but that we all must practice. Self-control is the ability to manage ourselves without external circumstances dictating our needs.

> IT MAY SHOCK YOU TO LEARN THAT YOUR SPOUSE (MOST LIKELY) WON'T WANT TO HAVE SEX ALL OF THE TIME.

⑮ GET A GRIP

Our bodies have real desires and they cause us to act out in pretty interesting ways. We can do things, strange things, without even knowing why. We call these behaviors "compulsive behaviors". There is no logical, conscious thought behind it; we acted on impulse. In moments like these, self-control seems to elude us, and even the best intentions fall flat. How can we change this?

Take someone who overeats, for example. A counselor will suggest that such a patient ask questions before binging on cheesecake at one o'clock in the morning. Questions like: "What am I feeling right now that makes me want to eat that? What am I feeling now, after I've eaten it?" The same logic applies to us with any of our compulsive behaviors. The point is not to ignore the urge and stop cold turkey, but to find the root in order to pull out the weed at the source.

What were you feeling before you looked at porn, before you sent that text message, or before you masturbated? We like to use a simple acronym in our community: HALT. Was I Hurting? Angry? Lonely? Tired? It's simple, but it's an easy way to remember to ask ourselves some basic questions. Were you feeling lonely, overwhelmed, angry, disconnected, or out of control? We will often act out in ways that make us feel powerful in the moment, but in reality, we're enslaved by internal circumstances. We're unable to understand that something in us is imbalanced, empty or just a little overgrown with weeds. In order to break these cycles and be truly satisfied, we must address ourselves point blank. It's time we get honest with ourselves so we can find our answers.

Working this out is something we do with God; we change our behaviors when we believe that we're capable of change. It starts with knowing who you are and who you are not. Believe that you can change and that God can redeem anyone. The Bible talks about working out our salvation, which means renewing our minds, surrendering our will, controlling our emotions, and retraining ourselves. It's true that around the age of twenty-five our brains are fully developed. However, it's also true that our minds are permeable and are always changing. The established pathways can be interrupted and rerouted. You know that saying, old dogs can't learn new tricks? Well, good news — we're not dogs, we're humans. Whatever the world wants to tell you about how much you're stuck in your ways without any hope for change, you can just scrap that. Right now. I'll wait for you as you get rid of that one.

In order for us to change culture and have a revolution in our own lives, we have to understand and respect the way we've been created. We need to know who God is. His ability is limitless.

> IN ORDER FOR US TO CHANGE CULTURE AND HAVE A REVOLUTION IN OUR OWN LIVES, WE HAVE TO UNDERSTAND AND RESPECT THE WAY WE'VE BEEN CREATED. WE NEED TO KNOW WHO GOD IS.

⑯ STOP, LOOK, LISTEN.

Sex itself is not the only time we begin to bond to things. As we've explored, our hormones are activated in many various ways. This is why it's important to have a handle on your thoughts, feelings and emotions, as well as your actions. There are three main areas that lead to connection, and they can have both a positive and negative influence over us.

LOOKING / LUSTING

Lust is defined as an overwhelming or intense desire or craving that motivates us to action. We lust after something. We know that this can be a serious issue. In the Old Testament, we were advised not to sleep with just anyone. In the New Testament, Jesus tells us that even lusting after someone can lead us astray. The Message version of Matthew 5:27 says, "You know the next commandment pretty well, too: "Don't go to bed with another's spouse." But don't think you've preserved your virtues by simply staying out of bed. Your heart can be corrupted by lust even quicker than your body. Those leering looks you think nobody notices — are also corrupt."

Okay, before you gouge your eyes out, let me explain that there's nothing wrong with your desire to look. Most of us are stimulated by visuals and looking with an appreciation for beauty is normal. God has wired us, and men in particular, to be stimulated visually. The reason for this is so that we would see our spouse naked and be completely attracted to them. Rest assured that no matter what stage of life you're in, your spouse will enjoy you (especially when you're naked). However, when it comes to people who aren't yours, there's a difference between looking and lusting after someone.

> WHEN YOU CHOOSE TO LOOK AT SOMEONE WHO IS NOT YOUR SPOUSE TO BECOME AROUSED BY THEM, YOU ARE LUSTING.

When you choose to look at someone who is not your spouse to become aroused by them, you are lusting. As a result, you create an intimate bond with them in your mind. Lust corrupts the intentions God had for our minds to remain pure, and for our eyes to see Him clearly. If the pure in heart shall see God, a lusting heart cannot.

As we explored in our section about the brain, we bond to the things that bring us pleasure. For example, if we consistently look at pornography, our thoughts stray into a dangerous territory that prevents us from seeing people in our life with a pure lens. We might begin to see people differently and think "pornographic" thoughts about them. This is a very real example of how what we look at can cause us to pervert reality.

Although both genders partake in this extracurricular activity, men in particular are affected by this. Approximately 100 million men in the U.S. and Canada accessed porn online in 2008, and by 2017, a quarter of a billion people are estimated to be engaging with such adult content from their mobile devices alone.[12] As this grows into a free, accessible and mainstream industry, it's crucial that we don't become desensitized to corrupt images of sex. The eyes consume so much for us, and sometimes completely unintentionally. You might not be able to control the first look, but you can absolutely control the second one.

THINKING / FANTASIZING

We know all too well that our thoughts are powerful. Proverbs 4:23 says, "Be careful what you think, because your thoughts run your life" (NCV). What we think about in our heart, we become. Again, we see this in Proverbs 23:7 which states, "For as a man thinks in his heart, so is he. As one who reckons, he says to you, eat and drink, yet his heart is not with you."

What happens when we take our thoughts too far? Fantasizing is effectively what happens when we leave the realm of possibility to wander in something idealistic. According to the Merriam-Webster dictionary, fantasy is defined as something that is produced by the imagination: an idea about doing something that is far removed from normal reality.

The key thing to notice here is that fantasy removes us from reality. Really, really far from reality. In general, women tend to do this more than men. We think that fantasizing isn't a big deal, and we might even hear ourselves say things like:

"Ryan Gosling is my fantasy dream husband. So, what's the big deal? I know it isn't real." The problem is that even though you don't really expect to marry Ryan Gosling, you still have an unrealistic ideal that isn't resolved. You think what you need is an alpha male with a six pack and a perfect haircut in order to be happy.

> WE'RE VENTURING INTO THE DANGEROUS TERRITORY OF FANTASY IF WE HAVE A "PERFECT LITTLE PLAN" BEFORE WE EVEN MEET SOMEONE.

We create worlds that aren't true, allowing us to fall in love, and yes, bond with something that isn't real. We become disappointed with what God gives us because it doesn't fit into our picture perfect ideal that we've been painting from a very young age. How many women imagine the perfect wedding as young girls? How about the perfect husband and the perfect happily ever after? You can thank Disney for this one. Is there anything wrong with having a vision for love and beauty? Is there anything wrong with imagining a life of happiness? Absolutely not. But people aren't perfect, and we're venturing into the dangerous territory of fantasy if we have a "perfect little plan" before we even meet someone.

How do I know that our culture has hooked us into a fantasy world? Soap operas, "reality" TV (which is, ironically, far from reality), romance novels, romantic comedies (and the list could go on), all suggest that we've become obsessed with a reality other than our own. These are scripted to sell you an ideal lifestyle, personality, and relationship. Did you know that the romance genre (romantic and erotic fiction) generated 1.35 billion dollars in 2013?13 84% of the readers are women, which tells us that women around the world are being stimulated by unrealistic romantic ideals.[14] We may think that the pornography industry is our biggest issue, but the romance genre actually generates more revenue than pornography.[15]

In real life and in real marriage, do you know what a sexy man looks like? A man who has a job and can do laundry. A man who can cook a good meal. A man who can change a diaper. That, my dear, is amazing. In my marriage, I like to say, "A man who empties the dishwasher is guaranteed to get laid." No joke.

I'm not saying you have to lower the standard of beauty that you have, but a man who loves you, is committed to you and isn't looking at anyone else is truly beautiful. The fantasy that tells you it must be roses, candles and limousines is lying to you. Yes, these are part of a wonderful expression of love but aren't (and shouldn't be) the pinnacle of romance.

How about a woman who respects you, supports you and makes you feel like a king? Guys, this is it. Find a real woman, not a piece of fiction. And listen, once you decide to spend the rest of your life with that person, they become the one. They become your type. They become what's sexy to you. What is your type? Your spouse is your type. My husband is my type. (I'm into skinny guys, if you'd like to know.) For a while, while I was pregnant four times, my husband was into pregnant chicks. Then he was into post-partum, girls. He's always been into blonds though.

All joking aside, fantasizing about other people communicates to your spouse that they aren't good enough; that they need to do more, be more, act more. Your spouse is (and will be) more than good enough. I promise. They will be the one because they become your one when you choose them. God created them in His image and you can trust that what you've been given will be more than enough. If it doesn't feel that way, you need to find the rest in Him.

TOUCHING

Touching is simply an experience of coming into close contact with someone. Touching is meant to stimulate something in us. Whether it be to build trust, or to arouse pleasure, touch is quite a powerful means for connection.

We tend to be quite particular in this area, allowing certain people to touch us and others not to. This is a good thing. However, when it comes to romantic ideals, we tend to think that touch should happen spontaneously. Stealing a kiss, grabbing someone's hand, taking someone into your arms media has done a wonderful job thinking that assertive or aggressive touch is the most romantic kind of interaction. They're all saying, "Go for it! What are you waiting for? They obviously want you."

Unfortunately, this has built up an unrealistic ideal in many of our hearts and minds. Many people think they want someone who knows what they want, and takes it. I mean, really goes for it. This is all well and good until someone crosses their boundaries, pushes too far, or takes what wasn't for sale. Or until they miss an excellent opportunity with a great guy or girl, because they didn't "act" the part.

We need to understand there are so many different ways to show that you want someone or make someone feel special. This is a real problem for young women who let men touch them because it makes them feel wanted and loved. They let men touch them because they think it's the only way to create a bond, or the only way they'll keep him around.

TOUCHING SHOULD NEVER EXCEED THE LEVEL OF TRUST YOU HAVE WITH SOMEONE

In reality, touching should never exceed the level of trust you have with someone. We must understand that touching (as we've explored earlier) bonds us to people, whether we want it to or not.

We shouldn't be stealing kisses. We should be asking for permission before we touch someone, especially if we're still building trust. I know, you don't think that sounds very sexy. But respect, honor and integrity should be sexy to us. The ability to have boundaries, enforce them, and have them respected by others is the pathway to healthy relationships.

Many of us think that being in love is synonymous with losing control. How many people have heard something like: "Oh, they're not in their right minds right now. They're just so in love!" This doesn't have to be the case. God certainly didn't want this for us. He didn't say, I've given you power, love and a sound mind except when you've fallen in love. When you're in love, you're just crazy. Those emotions are going to take over. Good luck.

I mean, it's a little absurd, but so many people think they have no control, no wisdom, no ability to think clearly when they're in love. Some of us have experienced that emotional haze (which can be a beautiful thing) but we should never be a slave to it. We've lost our ability to be Christ-like when we've given in to desire, ideals, and emotions. Our emotions aren't king. As we'll explain in the next section, our soul is no longer the ultimate source of truth because we have His Spirit living in us.

The reality is that touch is powerful. Premature physical intimacy will push your relationship to a place that it isn't ready to go. It's difficult to backtrack when you get to a level that can't be sustained. The only way to continue building connection at that point is to continue being physical. Many of us have experienced this: we feel disconnected if we're not being physically intimate.

Let me use an example. Let's say that you're in a relationship where there wasn't any real emotional intimacy established at the beginning, and, honestly, it was more physical than anything. Now, a couple months in, things aren't very exciting, and you realize that there's not much depth to your connection. Being physical with each other is the only way you feel close and connected. It will be very tempting to try to rekindle that spark, that powerful connection you once had, by throwing gasoline on the fire (making out, or crawling into bed together). In this scenario, I must warn you: this is a slippery slope that will lead to dangerous territory. Each time you use physical contact for intimacy and connection, you'll need to do something a little more risky or intense to get the same rush. Each time you'll burn out just as fast as before, leaving you bored and unsatisfied. It would be better to let the fire die out so that you can rebuild it on something substantial and enduring (like trust, healthy communication, and shared interests) than try to keep it going. Stepping back to reestablish boundaries isn't impossible, but it's easier to use wisdom, good communication, and a vision for success at the beginning to keep ourselves in line.

No matter what your personal stance is on holding hands, kissing, or other forms of physical touch, keep one thing in mind: everything from holding hands to sexual intercourse — all physical interaction — will release some level of chemical response in the body. As you choose and define your own boundaries, be kind to yourself. Know your point of arousal and protect it with all your might.

> **NO MATTER WHAT YOUR PERSONAL STANCE IS, KEEP ONE THING IN MIND: ALL PHYSICAL INTERACTION WILL RELEASE SOME LEVEL OF CHEMICAL RESPONSE IN THE BODY**

⑰ WALK THE LINE

When it comes to physical relationships, everyone (particularly everyone in the church) is asking: Where's the line? How far can I go while still remaining pure? What did God say about all of this?

The Bible never outlined most of this for us. The scriptures don't specifically say what we can and cannot touch, or what areas are off limits. Below the wrists and ankles? Nothing that's covered by clothing? What can we do when we're dating? What about when we're engaged? Though I can't give you specifics from the Bible, I can give you a little wisdom. The one place we see scripture talk about this is in Song of Solomon. Don't let the wildlife references throw you off — it's a powerful point:

> *Oh, let me warn you, sisters in Jerusalem, by the gazelles, yes, by all the wild deer: Don't excite love, don't stir it up, until the time is ripe — and you're ready (Songs 2:7, MSG).*

By the gazelles and wild deer? What is this? Calm down, it's really quite simple. Let me say it this way:

Let me warn you, dear beloved, Bride of Christ, in all gentleness — don't stir up a love, don't excite your body, don't go there, until the time is right and you can see it through.

There's nothing more tortuous than getting all hot and bothered and having to strain against your entire being, the way you were designed, and stop what you desperately want to follow through to completion. This is why my one concrete suggestion is that you learn what your point of arousal is, and save it for your wedding night.

> **LEARN WHAT YOUR POINT OF AROUSAL IS, AND SAVE IT FOR YOUR WEDDING NIGHT**

I would like to suggest that God put an internal line in each of us. No one can draw your "line" for you; it is determined by what turns you on, and what your personal convictions are.

I know that some of you are squirming in your seat right now, desperately hoping for more instruction than that. Why didn't God explain all of this in writing? Because He wants to be in relationship with you, not just give you rules. He wants to see you grow into maturity in Him. No child grew into a responsible adult just by following the do's and don'ts; we grow as we learn to think wisely and make good choices.

The reason God didn't give us the "Ten Commandments of Dating" is because our ability to be powerful in partnership with Him is more important than blindly living "by the book". God has given you the responsibility to make wise decisions for yourself. He loves watching you think and choose and grow, and learn from mistakes and wisdom alike. He trusts you. He is not worried about you slipping up. He gave us a Spirit that enables us to walk in power, love, and wisdom because He wants us to learn what it looks like to partner with Him as children, not follow rules like slaves. In this journey of discovering righteousness and holiness, He permits us absolute freedom in order to walk the tightrope of life confident that He is the net that will catch us when we slip.

In short, He wants relationship with us. It's okay if you're not sure what that means yet. Like any other relationship you have, understanding and trust builds over time. When it comes to sex, if you're wondering how far you can go, ask yourself what purity means to you. Does it mean virginity? Is it a list of yeses and nos? Or does it mean being close to Him? You'll have to find out what God is saying for you specifically and structure your life around that.

04 | SEX And NEEDS

By His divine power, God has given us
everything we need for living a godly life
2 PETER 1:3 (NLT)

⑱ HAVE YOUR CAKE (AND EAT IT TOO)

Remember the story of David from the last chapter? We left him in a very vulnerable place. Let's do a quick recap: He sees Bathsheba bathing, invites her over, sleeps with her, and then discovers she is pregnant with his child. Soon thereafter, unable to trick Bathsheba's husband into having sex with her, David hatches a plot to have him killed. It works. Bathsheba, grief stricken, mourns his death before accepting David's marriage proposal. She moves in with him and gives birth to their son.

It was time to move on with life, or so David thought. I'm sure he was mourning in his own way, probably hardening himself against those questions, the ones we all ask when we know we're guilty of something: Why did I do that? How did I let it go this far? This isn't who I am! I'm God's man! How did I fall this far? Unfortunately, when Nathan the prophet came to town, things got even more intense:

"David," Nathan started, "let me tell you a story. There once was a man who had nothing except one, small sheep, which he loved dearly. His neighbor, a very rich man, decided to throw a dinner party. Instead of using one of his own lambs, he stole and served up his neighbor's precious pet lamb. What do you think about that?"

David was furious. He couldn't believe the selfishness, the greed, the disrespect, the evil. "That man deserves to die! I have never heard of a man with less compassion! He needs to be taught a lesson! He needs to make it right! He must give back four times what he took!" He was shaking as he spoke, overcome with anger.

"David," Nathan said gently, firmly, with tears steady in his eyes, "You are that man."

Everything froze.

David was dumbfounded. His face drained white, then flooded with crimson embarrassment and rage. How did Nathan know? He was an adulterer. He was a murderer. And now the secret was out.

"...and because you have given the Lord's enemies a reason to mock Him, your baby will die. David, nothing is hidden from God."

Suddenly, David heard cries ringing through the palace corridors.

"My son!" he shouted anxiously. He threw open the heavy doors and started down the hallways.

For seven days, the fever never ceased. For seven days, David wept and fasted and prayed. He would not be comforted. He would speak to no one. In the silence, the servants could hear his petitions in muted soft tones, floating in the stillness:

*Look on me with a heart of mercy, O God, according to Your
generous love. According to Your great compassion, wipe out
every consequence of my shameful crimes. Thoroughly wash me,
inside and out, of all my crooked deeds. Cleanse me from my sins.
For I am fully aware of all I have done wrong, and my guilt is
there, staring me in the face. You're the One I've violated, and
You've seen it all. Whatever You decide to do with me is fair.[1]
But please, O God, spare my son!*

On the seventh day, everything stopped. The fever. The
fasting. The prayers. The child was dead. David, knowing
that his supplication could accomplish nothing more, got up,
showered and got dressed. After all, he had a wife to take
care of. Bathsheba and David found comfort in each other's
arms, and from that intimacy — bare, raw and honest before
God — came their son, Solomon. Under his leadership, the
whole nation of Israel would experience peace.[2]

In the days to follow, David was found in the temple,
worshipping. It is from his season of grief that we get one
of the most beloved psalms in history:

*Create in me a clean heart, O God; restore within me a sense of
being brand new. Do not throw me far away from Your presence,
and do not remove Your Holy Spirit from me. Give back to me
the deep delight of being saved by You; let Your willing Spirit
sustain me.[3]*

The good news is that God restored
David, and He can restore you.
In fact, 2 Samuel 12 tells us that
because of David's immediate
repentance in reaction to the
prophet's word, he was forgiven.
But that's the topic of the next

> **THE GOOD NEWS IS
> THAT GOD RESTORED
> DAVID, AND HE CAN
> RESTORE YOU.**

chapter; you're going to have to wait to hear more about that.

Like David, many of us are in painful cycles, or pits, if you will — relationally, mentally, emotionally, physically, or spiritually. Why? How did we land in the pit? I have found that oftentimes it's really quite simple: we had a legitimate need that we met in an unhealthy way.

A NEED IS SOMETHING NECESSARY.

For example, David stayed home when he should have gone to war. This is what he was made for, trained for, and born to do. When he stayed home, he exposed a need. What's a need? A need is something necessary. You're not going to do well without it being met. In this chapter, we're going to discuss the needs we have — body, soul, and spirit — and what we can do to get them met in a healthy way. Why is this important when it comes to our sexuality? Because when you get your spirit and soul needs met in a healthy way, your sex drive, or "physical needs", quiet down. When you have unmet emotional, mental, spiritual or even basic physical needs, your sex drive can be unmanageable and your decisions unreasonable.

So, what did David need? I don't know for sure, but I'd guess it was something in his soul — purpose, comfort, maybe adventure? Or maybe he actually forgot who he was; he was spiritually disconnected. Whatever the need was, I think it's safe to say that he made the same mistake that so many of us are still making today: He tried to go into the bedroom to get his soul or spirit needs met. He was longing for something on the inside, and felt like sex would fill the void. This is never a good plan, and it certainly didn't work out for David.

How do we live out an abundant life? How do we get free of haunting cycles, chronic, compulsive decisions, and the shame and guilt that so often follow? We learn to get our needs met. We learn to take care of our whole self — body, soul, and spirit. Keep reading and we'll start learning together.

⑲ BODY BUILDERS

In order to physically survive, our human body has four very basic needs: food, water, air, and shelter. All other needs we have (like the right outfit, transportation, or a gym membership) are secondary; you don't need these things to physically stay alive.

> IN ORDER TO PHYSICALLY SURVIVE, OUR HUMAN BODY HAS FOUR VERY BASIC NEEDS: FOOD, WATER, AIR, AND SHELTER.

If we meet all of these basic needs properly, we end up with living, breathing, healthy bodies. This is a pretty good place to start, right? Yes, there are other things that play into good health (such as exercise, good hygiene, and sleep), but getting these few needs met will keep us alive. If we abuse these needs, it can lead to physical illness, obesity, or anorexia.

Because our soul (mind, will, and emotions) is affected by our body (thank you very much, hormones), not taking care of our bodies properly can cause mental or emotional problems. An example of this would be how depression is sometimes brought on by a chemical imbalance in the body. Since depression is an emotional state that can be rooted in our physical experience, many doctors will even call it a mental illness. It alters the way we process information and form our thoughts. In a similar way, many of us struggle mentally or emotionally because we're not getting enough sleep. Any healthcare professional will tell you how important a good night's sleep is — and I can vouch for this.

I remember sitting in a pediatrician's office after having my second son, sharing with her how I was struggling, feeling totally overwhelmed. She listened and finally looked me straight in the eye, saying, "Well, it sounds like you have postpartum depression." As she said it, my eyes immediately filled with tears. I knew she was right. I needed help and that's what I was going to get.

I left the office that day and ran to my car. I called my friend's mom who, I remembered, was a Christian counselor in my area. I left a voicemail, explaining how I was struggling. I was surprised when she called me back within the hour. (As it turns out, when you're a new mom and they think you might have postpartum depression, they take you very seriously; they want to make sure you don't hurt your baby.) She made an appointment for me that same day.

To make a long story short, after the preliminary interview, she shared with me that I did, indeed, have postpartum depression. In fact, out of the fourteen symptoms she had listed, I had thirteen. I was shocked, yet relieved at the same time; somebody knew what I was going through. Someone was going to be able to help me. Being the "do-er" that I am, I was on the edge of my seat, ready to take whatever action she suggested. The first thing she told me to do? Sleep.

"Go home and get three good nights of sleep in a row and then we'll talk," she said. I was shocked.

"Do whatever you have to do. Get your husband involved, get your parents involved — just do whatever it takes. Sleep eight hours per night for three nights in a row, and then we'll talk."

It was then that I began to learn how important sleep is to the brain and function of the whole body.

Did you know that if you don't get a good night's sleep for three nights in a row, not only are you extremely exhausted physically, but you damage your ability to make sound judgments? This may be the reason why, sexually, we're out of control. What do we turn to when it's late and we're tired, wanting comfort and a release of stress? Sex. Porn. Masturbation. Why? It provides the necessary pleasure and comforts that our body is seeking, inducing feelings of security and peace. It's not meeting our true need (rest, safety, comfort), but it's an adequate, short-sighted solution (except for the side effects of shame, guilt, disconnection, and addiction).

We all need a bedtime. I have one, and I'm married, have my own house, and have four kids. Mine is ten o'clock every night. Do I do this because I'm a pervert and can't control myself? Absolutely not. I do it because I know what I need, and when I get what I need, my whole life feels easier.

WE ALL NEED A BEDTIME.

There's one other need that I didn't mention: **touch**. Physical touch may often be overlooked, but we have critical needs in this area. Did you know that newborn babies who don't get held can actually die, even when they get the rest of their basic requirements met?[4] Some of us feel like we're crazy because we feel the desire to be held; we feel the need to sit close to people, hold hands or get lots of hugs. I have good news for you — there's nothing wrong with you! If this is you, don't punish yourself by withholding touch or physical closeness from yourself and others. You were made to need it. (Of course, being too needy in any way can be a sign that something is off.) We were born to be in community, in close contact with other humans. Just find some healthy ways to get it. Spend quality time with family or friends, get a pet, or work in the church nursery. I know it sounds funny, but some of you may just need to hold some babies because it'll take care of your need for touch. It doesn't need to be perfect, just good enough to satisfy the immediate need.

If you're struggling with your sex drive, do a physical checkup: Are you eating well? Are you drinking enough water? Getting sunlight? Sleeping enough (and sleeping deeply)? Are you getting enough healthy touch? This may not be the root of your problem, but it's a good place to start. Take care of yourself. You're the only you you have and you are the only one responsible for yourself.

⑳ SOUL FOOD

Welcome to your soul — the aspect of you that is uniquely different from everyone else. Your soul has been with you your entire life, whether you were a Christian or not. It's the realm where every emotion we feel, every thought we think, and every desire and appetite we have dwells. Your soul is independent from your spirit and body, and has needs that must be tended to.

The Bible says in Psalm 84:1–2, "How beautiful are the places where you live, O Lord of all! My soul wants and even becomes weak from wanting to be in the house of the Lord. My heart and my flesh sing for joy to the living God." In this psalm, David is acknowledging that his soul has needs and without those being satisfied, he is weak. It has longings and desires; gaps that need to be filled. David gives us invaluable insight into the way we are as children of God, and allows us to see what is acceptable as we meet our needs. You might be surprised to learn that our soul needs things just like our body needs air, water, and food to live. So, without further ado, let's explore some of these needs and how to get them met.

> **OUR SOUL HAS THREE BASIC, UNIVERSAL NEEDS: INTIMACY, CONNECTION AND COMFORT.**

Our soul has three basic, universal needs: intimacy, connection and comfort.

Let's look at **intimacy** first. Intimacy means being close, familiar, and usually affectionate with another person or group. You could even break it down to spell it like this: in-to-me-you-see. It says it all right there.

Being known by people and by God isn't just a desire, it's a real necessity. If you are disconnected from others, you'll be lacking in certain areas, which can lead to feeling overlooked, overwhelmed, and unknown. These empty places will lead you to feel insignificant, meaningless, or even suicidal. Eventually, you may feel as though you shouldn't be on the earth and that if you left, nobody would notice or care. The enemy loves to target these lies directly at this unmet soul need. For many of us, it is our weakest spot — our Achilles heel.

There's a part of us that feels like intimacy is a luxury, and I want to say to you that intimacy is a need, not a want. You need intimacy in your life, and there are healthy ways to meet this need. It may not look ideal for you at first, but this chapter will explore those options for you.

INTIMACY IS ALLOWING SOMEONE TO SEE YOU AS YOU ARE AND LOVE YOU.

Intimacy is allowing someone to see you as you are and love you. It's the willingness to leave gaps in our hearts and our lives for other people to fill. You can't be a lone wolf or a one-man circus and be successful in this area.

Our first intimate connections are with our family. We start off as babies who rely solely on someone else's ability to hear us, see us, and listen to us. If we aren't seen or heard, we suffer greatly and our emotional growth is stunted. Why? Because this is a requirement in order to be healthy. Some of us didn't have guardians around to care for us, or we never knew our real parents. Regardless, God said He would put the lonely into a family.[5] Whatever needs you have for intimacy, God will help you meet them. Ask and you will definitely receive. Ask God to help you meet new people, to open up and to live without fear of being hurt. If you ask for bread, will He give you a stone?[6] No. In fact, He will give you even greater things just because you asked. He's that good.

It's important to make note (considering this is a book about sexuality) that it's easy to be misled in thinking that intimacy comes only through sexual or romantic relationships. For some of us, being intimate with someone may have always meant engaging in sexual activities with them, but God desires us to be intimate in other ways. Sure, we're all yearning for our fair share of make-out sessions and long nights of cuddling, but there are many ways to be intimate. Have you ever locked eyes with someone for a long period of time? I don't know about you, but that almost feels more intimate than holding hands. Try making eye contact with complete strangers. It's just uncomfortable for some people, like you're somehow invading their privacy. Sometimes it's in small, unexpected moments that we feel the most known.

We were made to be seen. No, maybe not by everyone we meet, but certainly by those we trust. As we begin to relate with one another on deeper levels of understanding (not just talk about the weather, but about our hopes, fears and dreams), we become known. We may feel simultaneously exposed and covered in this intimate exchange. It's a two-way street; allowing someone to hear your innermost thoughts, see you emotionally, baring all, and then allowing them to interact with you in the same way. This process begins to build friendships designed to last us a lifetime. Take David and Jonathan, for example.[7] Their friendship was marked by risk, loyalty, and vulnerability on both ends. This need for intimacy goes far beyond simply being present in your friendships — it's allowing yourself be fully known by others.

This also means that you can't rely entirely on one person, even if you are married or have a really, really close friend. It's a good place to start, but we must understand that one person cannot meet all of our intimacy needs. This means that we need to give to and share with a variety of people. Opening up to others may feel risky or painful at first, but know that it's worth the risk. We can only love to the extent that we're willing to be hurt. The deeper you let someone in, the bigger the risk is and the bigger the reward will be.

We have to be brave as we seek relationship, knowing that people aren't perfect. They are most likely going to disappoint us at one point or another. Jesus hung out with people He knew would reject Him, but loved and gave to them anyway. Of course, we must first seek Him for an intimate connection so that we can learn how to have healthy relationships with others. He didn't give us a need for intimacy so that we would suffer at the hands of irresponsible people, but so that we would depend on Him first and foremost. Intimacy with God will pave the way for healthy intimacy with other people in our life.

> **INTIMACY WITH GOD WILL PAVE THE WAY FOR HEALTHY INTIMACY WITH OTHER PEOPLE IN OUR LIFE.**

Another soul need we have is for connection. We need to feel connected; to know that our story is not an isolated story, and that we were born on purpose. We need to know that the baton is being passed from generation to generation, and our story links up with the eternal plan of God. We also need to feel connected in our hearts to people. This is similar to the need for intimacy, but will look a little different. Connection doesn't mean showing someone your innermost thoughts, but rather about helping others, being actively present, being aware of how others feel, and walking out God's plan for unity. It's a Philippians 2 "be humble and consider others more important" idea that allows us to lift and be lifted, influence and be influenced. We aren't just a single twig lying on the ground, we're the branch on a tree with other leaves, branches, fruit, buds, and roots. We are part of a great community. We were not made for isolation and independence, but to thrive within family.

> **BEING CONNECTED RELATES TO KNOWING THAT WE BELONG SOMEWHERE.**

Being connected relates to knowing that we belong somewhere. First, we can understand that we belong and are accepted completely by God — we have been grafted in to the vine, given access to life and love. But we also need to do basic things like make eye contact with people, have face-to-face interaction, smile at one another, help our neighbors, and carry one another's crushing burdens. We need to share the testimonies of our lives, our victories and triumphs, celebrate diversity of experience, and allow other lives to touch and teach us as we weave our stories together.

Part of meeting this need looks like finding people with whom you can go through life. Put yourself into a community of people who believe in you, sharpen you, and challenge you to become the best version of yourself. If you're struggling to feel connected, what can you do about it? Let me ask you some questions: Who knows you? Who speaks into your life? Who influences you? Are you taking care of yourself or are you hoping someone else is going to do that for you? Yes, we require help from others to meet this need, but first and foremost, we're responsible to govern ourselves well.

Proverbs 25:28 says, "He who has no rule over his own spirit is like a city that is broken down without walls." When our walls are broken and our foundation is cracked, the helping hands of others take us further than we could go alone. In the middle of a community, we are given the safety of others to build the right foundation, seal up the cracks, and keep out the bad. While discussing how to be in community, it's also important to remember how to have good boundaries. By letting the good in, and keeping the bad out, you indicate to those around you that you know you're a city worth protecting, and that your value is secure.

OUR SOUL NEEDS TO BE SOOTHED, REASSURED, AND COMFORTED.

This leads us into a third area which is a need for comfort. What does that mean? Our soul needs to be soothed, reassured, and comforted. The world is a hard place to exist in; Matthew 5:45 says that it rains on the just and unjust the same. This means we are all touched by pain, sorrow, rejection, and grief; by things in our world that hurt us and inevitably change us. Our need to be comforted in our soul allows us to feel safe and secure in an unstable environment.

Do you know what brings you a sense of comfort, happiness, and peace? Maybe it's slowing down, taking time for that cup of coffee or tea in the morning, or actually allowing yourself to get a massage once a month. Yes, I know, it's super spiritual. Why do we deny ourselves moments that bring us comfort? If your child just wanted to get wrapped in a blanket and cuddle with you, would you deny them this comfort? Why, as adults, do we feel like taking care of ourselves is the last priority? Maybe all it will take is buying new, soft bed sheets for the first time in 10 years. Or taking that vacation you've been dreaming about. Whatever it may be, think about what you take comfort in and realize that they are actual necessities for your soul.

Jesus told us that the Holy Spirit would be our comforter,8 because comfort is a requirement. We need to feel joy, peace, truth — these things calm the stormy waters of our soul when things aren't going well. Even if our external circumstances are trying, and we cannot have that cup of coffee or our "listening ear" is out of town, having comfort is still a promise. Matthew 5:4 tells us that we can be happy even when we're mourning, because we will be comforted. How do we receive this comfort? We receive it through our relationship with the Holy Spirit.

Remember, we were always meant to have the Holy Spirit working with us. John 14:16 says that we received another comforter (someone in addition to Jesus), one who will never leave us or forsake us. The word used also means advocate, counselor, redeemer. In John 7:38, Jesus said that whomever believes in Him will have streams of living water flowing from their innermost being. He is talking about the Holy Spirit who functions perfectly with our human spirit and soul. As the source of holiness and happiness, the Holy Spirit will abide with every believer forever. Just knowing that is a comfort in and of itself, isn't it? Knowing that God's Spirit lives in you, that He never leaves you, that there's nothing impossible because He is for you — this brings comfort when everything seems to be crumbling.

Many times we experience God's comfort as we watch (seemingly powerless) when things happen around us. We feel out of control, yet we feel God's ever-present love and a sense of hope. He doesn't need to use audible words for us to feel comforted in troubling times. In those moments, nothing changes and yet everything changes. Everything feels right inside of you even though you've lost your job, you're bankrupt, your dad stopped talking to you, or your girlfriend broke up with you. Whatever it is, we feel this comfort because the Holy Spirit is with us for this specific reason: peace that surpasses understanding. Unreasonable grace. Deep and profound joy that strengthens us when we would otherwise break under the weight of the world. These are God's promises to us.

It's true that in times of deep suffering and pain, we are comforted the most. In the Beatitudes in the Gospel of Matthew, Jesus explains that those who are persecuted are blessed, and those who feel as though they've lost everything will gain everything. There will be times when trying to comfort ourselves simply won't be sufficient; we are dependent on the

Spirit for this real requirement of comfort. Our soul needs the Spirit. We are to do nothing without Him.

We need to know that as His children, we can run to God and get what we need at any time, even as adults. When my kids are crying and need to be comforted, they will run to me to get that comforting cuddle or hug, whatever it may be. Once my little ones have felt comforted, they run off and carry on like nothing happened. Why? They got what they needed. That's it. A three year old isn't rejecting you when he doesn't want a second hug, it's just that he got what he needed, and then walked away feeling satisfied. That's what we do in our spirit — we get what we need and then we're fine for a while. We run to God and cry our faces off, and then get up and do the dishes. We need to be able to respect our need for comfort.

Some of us are completely comfortable doing this with God, but because of disappointment, pain, or past experiences, we won't allow others to come close enough to meet our needs. Some of us will deny it and act as if we're overwhelming people with our burden for connection. We may feel needy or unhealthy, but we're only hurting ourselves. If we will learn to get our need met in a healthy way by first courageously acknowledging we have a need and then meeting it quickly, we would be fine. Instead, we put on a brave face and sing God, You're all I need, the air I breathe, You're my everything! The truth is we need other people, too, but sometimes we just don't trust them.

Am I saying we should put people before God? Absolutely not. However, I am saying God put us in a family for a reason. Regardless of the circumstance, we are not made to live with fear towards others. If we are going to be satisfied, whole and healthy, we have to let go of fear and be honest about what we really need.

㉑ SEX NEEDS

Let's say that we're looking to get our needs for intimacy, connection, and comfort met. There is both an ideal way and an adequate way to get them satisfied. Let me show you what I mean.

Imagine I have a cup of water and a cup of ice. Both are water in different forms. The water represents the ideal way to get our needs for intimacy, connection, and comfort met: marriage, sex, and the perfect stud-muffin of our dreams with a perfect body. We believe that we absolutely need that water in order to get our needs satisfied. It's what we pray for and cry over. We're convinced we'll die of relational dehydration without it. We just won't be satisfied until we have that cup of water.

Then God shows up and offers you a cup of ice. He tells you that this will satisfy you; it's enough for the season that you're in. He's offering you friendships and a place in community. He knows it will meet your needs for now. It's not your ideal, but it's enough. If you take the time to build those relationships (let the ice melt), they will quench your "thirst". The Bible teaches us (Ecclesiastes 3:1–22) that God knows us and gives us what we need for the season we're in. Sometimes we just have to let go of our ideal for a little while.

> GOD KNOWS US AND GIVES US WHAT WE NEED FOR THE SEASON WE'RE IN.

I know what you're thinking: But, what about my need for sex? How will I get that need met without sleeping with my boyfriend or girlfriend?

Okay, let me tell you how to get your sexual needs met. Are you ready?

Sex is not a need.

Your "sex needs" aren't in that cup of water because sex is not a need. You need intimacy, connection, and comfort. That's what's in that cup. In order to be satisfied in waiting, we must surrender our entitlement (which we believe we can use to strong-arm God into giving us what we want, when we want it) and begin to trust His goodness and His timing. We need to become realistic about what our needs are. The whole world acts like this cup of water needs to be everything — supermodel partner, amazing sex, a wild party lifestyle. No, this water will satisfy the basic needs that you have in order to live well now.

Comfort, intimacy, and connection — that's it. Let's pull back for a hot minute and accept what our real needs are because if we get them met, our other "needs" (such as physical desires) will calm down and seem less demanding.

At this moment, most people wonder, "So, how then do I stay pure?"

Take care of the basics first. If you get your soul and spirit needs met, your "physical needs" will calm down. The reason we can be so sex-crazed and aroused all of the time is because we aren't catering to the real needs that we have.

Did you know that your soul responds directly to whatever you are feeding on? If your soul isn't getting what it needs, it gets hungry. It gets cravings. Your soul begins to ache, asking to be fed. Have you ever craved time with God? Longed for a phone date with your best friend? Desperately wanted to spend time by yourself? Felt like you had to go on a spontaneous adventure or you would die? If you ignore an appetite or craving, you'll end up starved and desperate, willing to be satisfied by any means necessary. You can't tell your body that its appetite doesn't matter and it doesn't need to be fed. The same goes for your soul. You might say:

"Well, I don't really need to eat."

Yes, you do.

"I'll just wait until I get a good meal."

No, you won't. What happens when you're planning on eating healthy meals but you don't eat all day? When all you have is cookies in the cabinet, what are you going to do when you get home? Let me tell you what you'll do. You are going to rip that box open and stuff them into your face. You may be repenting your whole way through it, but your body will be loving you because you've starved yourself to the point where it will be satisfied with whatever is around.

That's why it's a problem when we, for example, try to be pure but isolate ourselves, or ignore the feelings and desires we have. We don't let people into our world and our process, walking around like nothing is wrong. When we don't get those basic needs met in a healthy way, we get home and do something stupid. Like look at porn. Or send inappropriate late night text messages. Earlier that morning, were you planning on looking at porn when you got home? No. You had a good Bible study, you prayed, you asked God to help you, but you never got into community. Nobody knows you, nobody sees you, and nobody is connected to you. You didn't give anything of yourself to anyone all day, so now, when you are alone, you're going to meet that need as quickly as possible. Why? Because the struggle is real and that craving is pointing at something important.

THERE IS NOTHING WRONG WITH YOUR NEED FOR CONNECTION AND COMFORT.

There is nothing wrong with your need for connection and comfort. There's nothing wrong with wanting to feel satisfied, complete, and whole. Don't think you're the alone in this — the shame that whispers you're the only one will prevent you from opening up and asking for help. Don't ignore it; if you act like you don't need to eat, you'll eat the wrong thing when your appetite overtakes you. When your survival instinct kicks in, it will take any means to live.

The goal here is to get to the hunger before the hunger gets to you. We all understand that when we choose to be healthy at the beginning of the day, when we eat food before we're really hungry, we can resist whatever isn't healthy more easily throughout the day. If you have that green smoothie and eggs in the morning, you can resist the donuts at the office because you're not hungry anymore. What does that look like? If you're "binge eating" with pornography at night, maybe you need to learn how to be vulnerable in order to feel connected. Maybe you need to call someone you can trust in the evening so that you don't feel lonely. Whatever the case may be, it's learning to respond to those needs we've already explored in earlier sections. It's arriving at a place where we're comfortable opening up, and we find good accountability to help challenge, motivate, and encourage us. (We'll talk more about accountability later.)

Ask yourself good questions that get to the root of the issue: What do I need? Am I feeling truly connected to people in my life? How's my heart doing? Am I just stressed out about something? Have I been vulnerable with people lately? When you've been satisfied on the inside with good things, undesirable things won't look so enticing.

㉒ OUR HOUSE IS A VERY, VERY FINE HOUSE

This brings us to the third aspect of ourselves: our spirit. As much as we'd like to think that our spirit is like a perfect little God-robot inside of us that doesn't need anything, the truth is

WE ARE GOD'S CHOSEN TEMPLE AND WE MUST RECOGNIZE THAT IT'S OUR JOB TO KEEP A CLEAN HOUSE.

that our spirit has needs, too. We are God's chosen temple and we must recognize that it's our job to keep a clean house. Our bodies are a dwelling place for the Lord. How incredible is that? And our spirit helps us in the most significant way: it connects us with God.

You may recall from Chapter 3 that your spirit was dead until you invited the Holy Spirit to live inside of you. Remember? It's as though there's a deflated balloon inside of us that is designed to host the Spirit of God. We all have this place, this balloon, dwelling within. When we invited Jesus to be our Lord and Savior, and were baptized in His Spirit, the balloon was inflated. In that moment, we became fully alive. We began to hear God's voice, we began to want to do what's right, and the Bible says in Ezekiel 36:26 that along with a new Spirit, God gave us a new heart, new desires and a whole new reality. At that moment, the Spirit began to lead you. He says, "Come on baby, you can do this! This is how you were created. Don't give up now. I'll help you!"

When it comes to satisfying our spirit needs, we know that the Holy Spirit helps us. Romans 8:9 says, "But you are not doing what your sinful old selves want you to do. You are doing what the Holy Spirit tells you to do, if you have God's Spirit living in you. No one belongs to Christ if he does not have Christ's Spirit in him."

As much as we must satisfy our soul and body needs in order to live well, we also have another need above all else: a need for God. You have a "God spot" inside of you and if He doesn't live there, everything will be out of balance. No amount of success, money, or attention from cute people is going to fill the gap intended for God. When you allow Him in, everything aligns, and things start to make sense. 1 Corinthians 6:17 says, "But when you are joined with the Lord, you become one spirit with Him." This means that if we abuse or fail to meet our spiritual needs, we are looking to someone or something else to give us our identity, complete us, lead us in our purpose, or reveal our destiny.

Our spirit needs truth (Jesus) to cultivate this true identity. We need to deliberately seek God and the truths He speaks. Our inner man is like our compass; if it isn't functioning well, how will we get direction for our lives? Like a good gardener, we are instructed to take ownership over our own spirit. We must take time to bless our spirit, feed and nurture it, and give it what it requires in order to be fulfilled and free. We need to have a keen awareness over the health of our spirit and what our spirit man needs, just as a city needs fortified walls.

In Mark 14:38, Jesus reminded His disciples that the spirit has needs, too. When He said, "The spirit is willing, but the flesh is weak," He was telling them that our spirit can be ready, but if it isn't strengthened through prayer, it may not be able to help us overcome whatever physical temptations we have. This is why prayer and reading scripture is so crucial for the nourishment and edification of our spirit. We literally feed off of the word of God, verbal declarations, thanksgiving, and praise. Our spirit needs an atmosphere that will draw it to attention. That looks like peace and worship, prayer and intercession, joy and wonder.

Who is in charge of my body, soul, and spirit? Philippians 4:19 says, "My God will meet all your needs. He will meet them in keeping with his wonderful riches. These riches come to you because you belong to Christ Jesus" (NIR). Yes, God is taking care of you, but we also must come to Him to become aligned in truth.

GOD IS TAKING CARE OF YOU AND WILL FILL EVERY NEED YOU HAVE.

Ultimately, God is taking care of you and will fill every need you have. If He hasn't filled it, it may very well be that it's not a legitimate need right now. If it's meant to be filled and you've asked Him, then it's going to happen in the right timing. He may not fill it your ideal way, but it will be enough for the season you're in. If we are living with good core beliefs that help us to be healthy (remember our 5 Power Beliefs: we believe God, we trust God, we're powerful, we're honorable, and we're significant), then we can rest assured that God will take care of us. We will know that we are believing these truths when the urgency of meeting our own needs lessens. I may be hung up on the fact that right now I'm not getting that "water" I was promised, but when I choose to remember that God is good and will supply my needs, I will start looking for the other ways God has provided to help me through this season. The Holy Spirit helps us find the best option for our current circumstance.

㉓ JUST DO IT

Woah, Nellie. That's a whole lot of needs to think about. You may be wondering what life is going to look like for you now, hoping I'm going to give you some tangible, real life examples of what this looks like. Luckily for you, I am.

James 1:22 says, "Be a doer of the word." Everything we are to do in this life is supposed to be done in the name of Jesus, according to His word. We play a part in all of this, and we there is a certain amount of action required. As we've already explored, when it comes to following the ways of God, it's going to take a little more than just existing. The word "do" that is used in relation to this "doing the word" originates from the word creativity.[9] This means that we might have to get a little crafty when it comes to doing life in this society. Yes, Martha Stewarts of the world, get out your spray paint and your glitter glue — your time has come!

Okay, maybe not that kind of crafty. But in reality, if we are to be successful in any area, wherever we land, whatever job we have and people we meet, we must get a little creative. We each have a unique blend of gifts, strengths, and experiences that make us who we are. There's no benefit to pretending otherwise, and there's no personal success in trying to be someone you're not.

The way I do life with God might not look the same as anyone else. What gives me a sense of comfort or connection may be different from you. How I get my needs met will depend on the kind of things I enjoy. Whether you get up to pray at sunrise, evangelize on the streets at one o'clock in the morning, or care for the elderly, there are many ways to act on your faith and live out His commands. Your ability to get the nourishment you need for your soul and spirit is simply going to look different from mine. It's based on your own unique concoction of strengths, gifts, and life mission. If you learn to be in charge of yourself, God will provide a way for all of your "essentials" to be met in a healthy way. First, it's up to us to steward this creativity in finding ways for our human needs to be met on earth . In order to thrive and live victoriously, we must have some strategies for success. This begins with knowing ourselves.

> **IN ORDER TO THRIVE AND LIVE VICTORIOUSLY, WE MUST HAVE SOME STRATEGIES FOR SUCCESS.**

Let me use myself as an example. I have a need to connect with God (as we all do). I am a spiritual being, and I need to hear from Him, as well as feel known and loved by Him. Back in my teen years, I was part of a Christian summer program. Part of our daily requirement was to take our journal, go sit out in nature, and listen for God to speak. It was the most frustrating exercise I have ever endured. Most of my journal entries said something like, "God, I can't hear you. Where are you? Are you even listening? I can't hear you. This is a waste of time." I'm sure that many of us can relate to that feeling — it's like the heavens are brass. No matter how long I sat there, nothing happened. My mind wandered to everything non-spiritual, from what movies were coming out to what I was going to eat for lunch. It felt like the connection just wasn't there.

As I got older, I realized some of the typical ways to connect with God just wouldn't work for me. No matter how long I spent in my perfect chair with my fuzzy blanket and cup of coffee, I just wasn't going to hear from God. That's not how He talks to me. I had to get creative and try different things. Instead of going to a quiet place, I'd go to a coffee shop. Instead of focusing really, really hard, I'd just keep my heart open to God and listen as I went about my day. I began to hear more clearly and feel more connected than I ever had in those quiet times on a mountainside.

Now, as a mom, I have to be even more creative. Some days I may not be able to get my ideal "cup of water," or even my enough-for-now "cup of ice". Some days, all I will get is an apple. An apple may not be water, but it contains water. In fact, an apple is eighty four percent water. This is enough to satisfy my thirst for a time.

I may not have a lot of time to read my Bible, like I did in my single years, but I keep my heart open and I hear God talk to me through my children, through circumstances, and through songs on the radio as I'm driving. I often say that I meet God between the washer and the dryer; my connection time with Him is in the midst of chores and errands. All I need is one good worship song on a Sunday morning (before I have to run to the nursery), or one timely, encouraging word from a friend. It may not be ideal, but I feel fulfilled. It's not water, but it's an apple. It may not be a full church service or an hour alone with my Bible, but there is enough spirit-to-Spirit connection in it to satisfy my need for today.

There are many ways people connect with God: music, reading, prayer, art, dance, journaling, or being in nature, just to name a few. If reading your Bible doesn't seem like enough, don't stop reading, but try something new as well. Try a creative expression like painting  or sewing. Get outside and listen and look for God in nature. Do something with your hands like help your dad work on his car or restore an old chair you found at a thrift store. Talk with people and listen for God's voice in what is being said. Be open to Him connecting with you in unconventional ways. You may be surprised at how you begin to hear Him in profound ways.

Another one of those basic needs that I have is one for intimacy. Ideally, I may want to get all of this attention from my husband — mentally, emotionally and yes, sexually. But the truth is that Ben doesn't have time to cater to my every need. He works. He takes care of our family. He works on the house. He runs errands. He travels. He needs to eat and shower and sleep. After getting married, I realized that he was not going to be able to give me everything I wanted; I would have to find other ways to experience intimacy. Some of this was met through my friends and family, and some came through unexpected sources.

When we had babies, I was surprised to find that my kids helped meet my need for intimacy. When I got to hold, talk to, and be close with my boys, I found that my needs for touch and emotional connection were greatly fulfilled. Some of us feel like we're very lonely or need more physical affection; start working with the children's ministry or in the nursery at church. Volunteer at an animal shelter. Join a sports team. Do something where you can just be in close physical proximity with people. Join a book club or small group where you can have deep or open conversation. Be creative. It may take time to find the perfect fit for you and your needs, but there are solutions if you'll think outside the box.

We each have many different needs and some are stronger than others. This is somewhat dependent on your personality. Some of us are introverts; we don't need much time with people, but we need good quality time with people. We don't feel lonely very often, just when we are misunderstood, or don't have any really close relationships. Some of us are extroverts; we thrive on time with people, love to be the center of attention and love to hear affirming words and encouragement. We may need more time with people if we are going to feel known. We all need connection, but the amount of connection you need and the form it will take will be specific to you.

Some of us need adventure. Our need could be met by going on a hike, taking a trip to a foreign place, or beginning a new friendship. Some of us need calm and peace. We might find it internally, reading a good book, sitting by a creek, or in sharing our heart with a close friend. Some need a strong sense of direction and purpose, while others thrive on spontaneity. You get my point. We may not need it in every area of our life, but just in one or two areas. If you're on this journey, begin by brainstorming with a friend or mentor: What do I need to thrive? How can I get my need for this met? Take the time to learn about yourself then begin the process of giving yourself what you need.[10]

As we become "doers" of the word, creatively pursuing God, connecting with people and acting in faith to love others, we begin to align with the vision God has for our lives. As we become more aware of our individual selves, we become people with self-restraint, proper boundaries, and focus for the future. Every day is an opportunity, an invitation, to show up, live with a vision, and be victorious, no matter what.

Jesus gave us an example of what this lifestyle looks like. He said that He only did what He saw the Father doing.[11] This means that He tended to what was in front of Him, what was necessary for the moment, and what was part of a greater plan. It's almost as if Jesus had a vision for His life and for humanity that kept Him focused.

> PART OF PARTNERING WITH GOD'S VISION FOR YOUR LIFE IS TRUSTING HIM, AND LEAVING ROOM FOR HIM TO NUDGE AND GUIDE YOU.

Part of partnering with God's vision for your life is trusting Him, and leaving room for Him to nudge and guide you. We're not doing it our way, independent from the vine, rather we're surrendering our will as we stay attached to the source of life. As we seek the things that satisfy us, we may need to allow God to remind us of the season we're in so that we can stay focused. If He says, "Hey, stop dating for a while so that we can work on you," you will have grace in your life to do what He's doing. Perhaps His desire is to weed out some of the unhealthy appetites, or starve some addictions. Of course we know that we're not bound by those things anymore, but He knows that if you don't feed the beast, it will lose its strength.[12]

The Bible says that our "old man" (2 Corinthians 5:17 refers to this old man as our old ways) will lead us to death. Being victorious in this life, even as we are seeking to satisfy our own personal needs, means that we must see ourselves from the perspective of the cross. Jesus' death and resurrection meant our death and resurrection. When we are born again, it's like God was saying: "You can't do it like that anymore. Let's try it this way instead. Slow down and let me be your balance. Let me lead you into freedom and truth. Let's begin to put some self-restraint into you so that the boundaries I've given you will protect you and lead you into life."

Don't worry if you feel like God is slowing you down and putting some training wheels back on. 2 Timothy 1:7 says, "For God did not give us a spirit of timidity (of cowardice, of craven and cringing and fawning fear) but he has given us a spirit of power and of love and of a calm and well-balanced mind and discipline and self-control" (MSG, emphasis added). We know that God disciplines those He loves, and His intention is always for us to be whole. It's His kind nature to give us parameters, to help us have boundaries, and to help us become strong.

It's a journey. Living a powerful, healthy, and balanced lifestyle takes time to learn. If we effectively feed our spirit and actively "do" the word of God, we're setting ourselves up for wisdom, growth, and success. You can develop healthy patterns now that will last with you well into old age, and through any trial that comes your way. You can live empowered and free with a community of people and the hosts of heaven standing on the sidelines cheering you on as you run. When you live a spirit-led life, purity isn't just something you do, it's something you are. Godly isn't what you do, it's who you are. Filling the God-given human gaps in you with wholesome nutrition, catered exactly to suit your unique self, is vital to your well-being.

05 SEX ~~And~~ RESTORATION

I may not be where I want to be, but thank God I am not where I used to be!

JOYCE MEYER

㉔ RIPPING OFF THE BAND-AIDS

"Today's going to be a very serious and personal topic. I have to be honest — we never repeat a topic on the show and the only reason we are sticking with this topic is because of the deluge of responses we received from you. You guys went crazy! Our twitter feed, Facebook wall — you guys left me messages, and it was like you had to tell me, 'this topic is so important!'"

Her raspy voice buzzed through my speakers as I settled in to my long drive to L.A. This podcast seemed juicy and I wanted in on it. I could almost feel myself leaning in as I drove. My speed increased, as did my interest.

"Today our topic is body image! But before we dive into the topic and hear from our expert, I want to play back some of the voice messages I received from you. And, yes, I listened to each one! Thank you. Thank you. Thank you, you brave souls — my lifers!" (My lifers: an affectionate term Charlene calls her loyal listening audience.)

The music began and quickly spiraled into a medley of voice messages, both male and female, sharing their stories of how they lived through painful body image narratives. It wasn't until I heard one girl's voice that my eyes fill with tears, beginning to imagine the horror she had endured. "My Dad made up songs about us. About our weight, I mean. He would sing them about us." She went on to sing the song which rhymed her name with a door and not being able to fit through one. It was horrible. It was cruel. It was eerily memorable and I could hear the crippling tone in her voice as she sang. The little girl was still alive inside this grown woman and, after all these years, the songs continued to haunt her. Time had done nothing to ease the pain. As quickly as her voice appeared, she had disappeared, but the thousands of us listening on the other end would not easily forget her story or the painful melody.

In this life, things aren't always fair or even kind. It's hard to live in a broken, fallen world. It seems that this brokenness spins in cycles without much hope of getting out — a fearful, insecure person has children, torments these children, who then grow up to be fearful, insecure adults. In the face of torment, bullying, disappointment, we've all experienced a series of cuts and bruises that go deeper than the skin.

We've all felt this to some extent — pain that stunts our growth like a broken leg that just won't heal. Except this pain is not physical; it's emotional. What happens when we have these wounds: the beatings that we didn't deserve, the manipulation, the deceit, the broken promises, the songs that haunted us? Well, without any help, we make ourselves a little home there. We think these pits of pain are normal, inevitable, part of us. Or, better yet, we use convenient methods to cover up the pit to pretend it's not there. Like Band-Aids over bullet holes, our attempt to cover them won't suffice, yet most of us slap them on and carry on. Beneath an "everyone hurts", or "forgive and forget" mentality, we are running around like shattered vases held together with pieces of tape.

Forgive and forget — we've all heard that phrase, right? How about "time heals"? That's a popular one, too. But neither of them really help us. It seems that I'm not the only one who thinks so, either. Rose Kennedy once shared, "It has been said, 'time heals all wounds.' I do not agree. The wounds remain. In time, the mind, protecting its sanity, covers them with scar tissue and the pain lessens. But it is never gone."

The story about the father who sang songs to his daughter, causing deep insecurities and body image issues, is one that rings all too familiar for many of us. Perhaps it's something different for you — a bully at school, a neglectful family, a broken promise, or a story of abuse. Regardless, we've all felt the pain of being cut deep: mentally, emotionally, spiritually, and sexually.

When it comes to sex, we're trying to understand what is good for us, what is right, or what to even talk about. Our society is still clawing its way out of a pit that we don't understand is even there. It's almost as if these wounds on our sexuality have become so common-place that we only look for temporary ointments rather than miracles of healing. As we scramble to recover from the effects of the Fall, we run in every direction in an attempt to solve this issue of sexual sin. Silence? Saturation? Liberation? It's-my-body-I'll-do-what-I-want-with-it thinking? "I was born this way" chanting? How do we get real freedom? How do we deal with objectification? Sexism? Abuse? As we check something off the list, it's almost as if another thing is added on. In an endless cycle, our world revolves around sex in one capacity or another.

What can we do about it? As a society, we are only just starting to have the conversation. Abuse victims break the silence, awareness campaigns are launched, and people become more informed, but we still have a long way to go. When it comes to the wounds in our lives, change may not be as simple as protesting or changing laws. Something, someone, may have impacted you deeply and that place needs to heal. We need to become whole as individuals if we're going to be whole as a society.

The woman from the podcast had grown up, lived life, moved on, but the song remained hidden deep inside of her, a swan song just ready to be sung once more. As our world attempts to "carry on". We try to forget memories of abuse, trauma, loneliness or regret, we use medication, alcohol, drugs, television, addictions, habits, projects, social media, work, even sex itself, as convenient Band-Aids that poorly deal with the issues of our soul. Yes, we look normal on the outside. But inside we are like an old scratching post with bits of cat-claw still stuck between the grain.

Why do we do this to ourselves? It seems that we've gotten quite good at finding temporary solutions for deeper problems. We're a big Band-Aid generation. But we don't have to be.

What if God could go back and heal those places? What if He could touch the scars of memory and smooth them over, leaving those pains undetectable? The shame, the confusion, the memories, the trauma, the unforgiveness, the regret. Luckily for us, we don't have to wonder if healing is even possible. With Jesus, it's not a matter of if; it's a matter of when. When is it a good time to let Jesus in to heal wounds? As they say, there's no time like the present. It's time to rip off the Band-Aids and look at ourselves from the perspective of redemption and grace. It's time to let the wounds breathe and be tended to. After all, no wound ever healed well by being ignored, covered up, or hidden from medical attention.

It's time for us to live like we believe that the truth will set us free.

The great truth is that we don't have to stay here if we don't want to. We don't need to ignore it in order to move on. We don't have to pretend we are stronger than we are. If you are feeling uncertain or helpless in the face of your pain, be encouraged in knowing that when we are weak, He is strong.

Sometimes the hardest part in the process of revealing wounds and hearing the truth is that we are face-to-face with our inadequacies. Face-to-face with places where we've fallen short or believed a lie. Places a little broken and a little messy. Little pits that became familiar and comfortable. But if we, like King David, can look our failure in the eye, push through, not submitting to regret, shame, or guilt, we'll find restoration waiting for us in the arms of Jesus. If we allowed the wound to just exist, maybe it would heal. Maybe it won't even leave a scar. Not only is God in the business of redemption, healing, restoration and making all things new, He's the expert.

Many of you are reading this, uneasy, feeling the ache of old wounds. Some of you are even trying to push those feelings down right now. Some of you are celebrating, remembering your own journey to wholeness. Wherever you're at today, I encourage you to press into this chapter. There will be grace for you, no matter if you're acknowledging your pain for the first time, or if you've been healed for decades. If you're just starting out, be gentle with yourself. Take it one step at a time. If you've already gone through healing and restoration, it's imperative for you to learn how to help others connect with themselves and with God, too. The earth is waiting for us to be both salt and light in order to bring healing to a broken world! Be bold. There is something waiting here, just for you.

Where do we start in all of this? Somewhere. Anywhere. Let's just start. You've never been here before, and that's okay. Be kind to yourself. Be real and honest. It's the first step in any journey of healing — admit that there's a problem, a lie, or a weak place that needs strengthening. Grab a journal, a pen, a comfortable place to sit — and get ready for something amazing to happen.

㉕ THE IMPORTANCE OF BEING EARNEST

Before we get to the places that require healing, we must learn to become a little more raw with God. Being raw looks like being more exposed than you may be used to. He's not expecting us to come to Him all cleaned up, with our hair brushed, in our Sunday best. If He's not afraid of our pain, our sin, or our so-called failures, why hide from Him as though He is? Why not go to our great Healer first?

In the Psalms, David is about as raw as it gets. I don't believe there is anyone else who is quite as authentic as David was when he prayed. Whether it's feelings of anguish, excitement, longing, or fear, David brings his whole heart to God's table.

In Psalm 51, David said something interesting that gives us an indication of what it might look like to ask God to help us. He said, "Renew a steadfast spirit in me." Here, the word renew implies a restoration for David's ability to be strong and steadfast. The word restoration means this: the action of returning something to a former condition; of reinstating it back to its original form or function.

What? Does that mean that David admitted that something wasn't right? Yes, it seems so. It also appears that he approached God with a teachable heart and a desire to change. (Remember how he immediately repented when Nathan the prophet confronted him?) In asking for a renewed, steadfast spirit, he's asking that all things that were taken, touched, or emptied, would be returned to their original design through restoration.

In a moment of vulnerability, David admits that there are some fears and insecurities that he wants — no, he needs — to be renewed. In the Moral Revolution translation, we would say it something like this:

> *"God, take me back to how I was created as a sexual being: pure, without shame or condemnation. I don't want to loathe my past or my so-called lack of purity. I want to be the child you created me to be."*

In this verse, we already know the word renew implies restoration, but did you know that there are roots here that imply something is being repaired, like polishing an old sword until it shines?1 Our renewal is like being polished until we're gleaming. Looking a little further,

OUR RENEWAL IS LIKE BEING POLISHED UNTIL WE'RE GLEAMING.

the word steadfast is the Hebrew word niphal which means to be firm, stable, established; securely determined and enduring. It's as if David's saying, "In this time of restoration, I pray that you would help me to continue polishing this part of me; that I would have an endurance that would last me through this season, until your perfect work is complete within me."

Of course, this doesn't usually happen immediately. Although we can be touched by God with miraculous and instantaneous power, the process of healing and renewal is exactly that: a process.

Practically speaking, if you're a little dull, it will take some time to get you looking shiny again. Remember, we've been given the perfect Spirit of Jesus which makes us spiritually spotless and clean, but the rest of us still needs some TLC. When we accept that Jesus paid for it all, we can get to work and live from the inside out.

It may help to get your journal and write down the places where you want to see restoration. Write down what you want to see happen, and what you believe God can do. Just as David did, open up your heart and articulate your desire for strength, hope, healing, and power. Give yourself permission to have unedited hope. Hope to think about the possibilities without restraint. This will serve as your hope manifesto as you walk through the valley, so to speak. Where are you a little rusty, dull or lifeless? What would it look like to be bright, shiny, and glimmering? To be steadfast, renewed, and walking in power? Give yourself a vision and allow God to show you what He wants to do.

㉖ SHINE BRIGHT LIKE A DIAMOND

The first Band-Aid we want to remove is the one we put over our spirit. Many of us have been wounded in this area because of our choices — because of our sin. I'm writing today to tell you that there is hope for you. God is absolutely able to restore you spiritually.

Let's start here: premarital sex, or other unhealthy sexual behaviors, affect our spirit because it is a sin. The Bible tells us that it's a sin against God and against our own body. Many of us are aware of its effects: we feel ashamed, guilty, dirty, or separated from God. We feel like we have to hide, particularly when it comes to sex, because it feels far too big to bring to God. Sometimes, it feels too big to even talk about. So, we hold ourselves back from the One who can make it right.

Where we get messed up is in our understanding of sin and separation from God. In the Old Testament, when the Israelites sinned, it separated them from God, and only offerings and sacrifices reconnected them.[2] Before we believed in Jesus, we too were separated from God by our sin.[3] But here's the good news — Jesus made the 'once-and-for-all sacrifice' for us, so that once we choose to believe in Him, it is impossible for God to separate Himself from us.[4] When we choose to sin, we are turning our back on God, and this causes our disconnection. Our fellowship with Him is broken. But this is not God turning His back on us, as we may classically believe. It is us turning our back on Him. He is always ready to receive us when we are ready to come home and make things right.[5]

How do we make things right? Repentance. It is changing your mind in such a way that you make a 180 degree turn, with remorse, from sin to God. Repentance instantly restores our connection with God.[6] It's not like waiting around all day for the cable guy to come and

REPENTANCE INSTANTLY RESTORES OUR CONNECTION WITH GOD.

hook up your TV and Internet. You know, they say they'll come sometime between 8am and 2pm, but there's no guarantee they'll actually show up. It's not like that with God. No mess, no waiting period, just done. Or, in His words, it is finished.

God responds to our initiation; He doesn't want to force you to do anything. But He also doesn't just wait around for us to come back. He stands at the door of our heart and knocks with patience, gentleness and, yes, sometimes conviction. He waits for us to open up for Him.[7] In fact, He is so ready to respond that when we simply turn our thoughts toward Him, reconnection begins.[8] Remember: extravagant, undeserved forgiveness is God's thing.[9] So, even if you don't think you're worth it, or deserve it, know that He's ready to give it whenever you're ready to receive. And know this: His mercy and grace does such a good job that when He's done with you, it's as though it was never an issue to begin with. You get a second chance. You get your power back. You're no longer doing it on your own.

Our need to be connected with God goes beyond sin and separation in a relational sense. We need to stay connected to our source, because He gives us the power we need. Without Him we are ineffective and unable to accomplish what we are called to.

Imagine yourself as a lamp. You were designed to bring light to the world, help people navigate dark paths, and bring warmth and comfort to your home. Now, you have a problem. You've been unplugged from the power outlet; you've disconnected yourself from your source of life. The outlet is there, only inches away, but you're not plugged in. What good can you do now? Sure, you're beautiful, you have a nice bulb, you have all the equipment you need to illuminate your environment, but if you're unplugged, you're not good for much.

As Christians, our relationship with Jesus Christ is much the same. Our access to the Source never changes, but our willingness to stay connected does. According to John 15:5, without our connection with Him, we can do nothing. This is why it is so crucial to activate our will and choose repentance and reconnection. It's not hard. In fact, it only takes a moment.

HE IS READY FOR YOU, EVEN NOW, WITH OPEN ARMS.

Remember, He is not far away. He will never leave you or forsake you. He is ready for you, even now, with open arms.

If it helps you, speak this aloud or write it down in your journal. Tell Him how you're not interested in staying the same, or holding on to the pain anymore. Write for a bit about how you used to be, how you used to think, or what you were holding onto. Next, take time to write about how that is all going to change, how it will be different. Let Him fill your words with hope and vision for the future. What does it look like to stay connected to His

Spirit? To be Spirit-led? To be constantly plugged in to the source of life? Allow yourself to really dream and imagine what this would look like. Invite Him to help you become that person.

㉗ BREAKING BAD (BEHAVIORS)

In the beginning, before God filled the cosmos with light and wonder, the universe was formless and void. There were no mountains, no laughing children, no Nicaraguan pour over coffee — yes, it was a pretty bleak place. And then, God filled it. With what? Well, to be precise, with seasons, symmetry, numbers, sounds, with life.

God created everything to exist in motion, in cycles, and in patterns. These cycles create patterns of consistency for growth to take place; they are a requirement for sustainability. The moon influences the tides in their cycle of rising and falling, in a dance of giving and receiving, of life, of change, of growth. The seasons occur in cycles because nature requires each one in order to thrive. Our sleep consists of cycles, alternating between two states of rest. God created everything around us deliberately as a delicate circle of life. As we know, cycles can be positive structures in our lives, but when the wrong pattern takes hold of us, they can also weave us into destructive lifestyles.

If you've ever been stuck in a cycle of depression (and I have) or addiction, you will understand what this pattern looks like. In those moments, it feels like we've lost control, feeling powerless, hopeless, and uncertain about ourselves. We often stop believing God for His hand in our life. When it comes to breaking cycles, we need to find out which cog in the wheel

WHETHER YOU REALIZE IT OR NOT, SEX CHANGES THE WAY YOU THINK ABOUT YOURSELF AND THE WAY YOU VIEW THE WORLD.

is stuck before we can get the others moving. Oftentimes, if we've engaged in premarital sex or other harmful sexual behaviors, we've already started looking at the world differently. Whether you realize it or not, sex changes the way you think about yourself and the way you view the world. It affects your soul — thoughts, emotions, and decisions — and because of its vulnerable nature, it opens us up to all kinds of lies.

So, these little lies that form over time jam our gears and prevent us from moving forward. Behaviors come out of belief systems (based on lies or truth) which need to be resolved before any behavior is corrected. How do we do that? You guessed it — it begins with being honest with ourselves in order to see where the problematic areas are.

In this section, we're going to explore some of those raw places in order to break some bad behaviors. By exposing any lies that prevent healing from taking place, we can put them to death and start creating new cycles of life.

As we learn how to apply the right ointment (truth) with a little elbow grease, these places of pain will start to heal quite nicely. Before you know it, you'll be walking in powerful kingdom mentalities about God, yourself and about sexuality. It may help you to write down these lies as we go through them, or to write down your own — whatever lies you feel are holding you down. Ask God: What's the lie I am believing? What areas do you want to target today?

LIE: I'M NOT WORTH THE WAIT, COMMITMENT, OR PROTECTION.

"I'm damaged goods. No one will want me. Why would I save myself now if I've already had sex? I was abused; I'm dirty and disgusting. I'm not pure, why would any good man pick me? If I get married someday, I'll probably just end up divorced; marriage doesn't ever last."

That's what this lie sounds like going through our minds. We believe that our value has been stolen or lost, and we deserve whatever we get. Maybe we think that we deserve to be punished, to live in pain, or to suffer. We don't deserve unconditional love — we

> **DEEP DOWN WE BELIEVE WE'RE GOING TO GET HURT OR EVENTUALLY ABANDONED, AND WE'D RATHER BE IN CONTROL OF HOW IT HAPPENS.**

couldn't even receive if it we wanted to. So, instead of walking into our new identity and into our second chance, we walk back into the arms of whatever robbed us, hurt us, disabled us, or ambushed us. And then, if we do get married, we sabotage our relationship. Deep down we believe we're going to get hurt or eventually abandoned, and we'd rather be in control of how it happens. This is how some women end up in prostitution. This is how men stay with abusive, controlling, manipulative wives. This is how we turn ourselves over as free-prey to the enemy.

If you identify with this thought, you need to know it is a lie from the pit of hell. If you get anything out of this book, let it be this: when you come to Christ, He makes all things new. He gives you good things. You're worth it. No one can take that away from you. You are pure, spotless, holy (that means set apart from this world). You are a new creation. There is nothing left of that old person in you. (See Chapter 2 for more identity truths.)

If you repented two minutes ago, you are not who you were three minutes ago. Yes, you may need some time to walk out your new-found freedom, but in that moment, everything changed. God is able to give back to you immeasurably more than the enemy ever stole from you, and more than you gave away.

LIE: GOD IS NOT TRUSTWORTHY

"Why would I wait for 'God's best' when I have had someone good enough? I don't think that at my age, with my experiences and my history, God is going to make my dreams come true. I'm going to make it happen for myself. I followed God, but He didn't give me what I wanted. He keeps making my life harder, and I'm done with it. I'm going to take control over my life and be happy."

Often, this lie isn't quite as blunt as what is written above. It can be a sneaky, subtle serpent whispering sweet nothings in your ear, telling you that you have to stay in control of your life. Do what's best for you no matter what. When something unexpected or disappointing happens, this lie pops in disguised as a "survival instinct." Maybe you thought your spouse-to-be was God's will for your life, and then suddenly they called off the wedding. Maybe you thought your parents were going to stay together, or that your loved one was going to live. Under the weight of emotional distress, we take our eyes off of God and put our hands back on the reins. We suddenly question whether or not God is going to crash-land our life. With this little lie, circumstances try to enforce the thought that God isn't going to take care of us.

> USUALLY THE CATALYST FOR CEASING TO BELIEVE GOD IS SOME SORT OF DISAPPOINTMENT IN OUR LIVES.

Usually the catalyst for ceasing to believe God is some sort of disappointment in our lives. We start analyzing things, thinking that God's motives aren't always right or good for us. When we don't believe God, or trust Him, we immediately begin to search for a replacement. Most often this is a subconscious choice. We try to find people to take care of us, or we fill our lives with things that bring us a sense of comfort, peace, or control. This is where the destructive cycle creeps in. Whether it's masturbation, drugs, hard partying, or unhealthy relationships, the negative cycle begins when we replace God by choosing to meet our needs our own way, by ourselves.

Disappointment with God will cause offence against Him. He encourages us to process our disappointment with Him freely and openly. He is not afraid of our pain. Believe Romans 8:28 when it says that God always works things out for those who love Him. That includes you.

LIE: GOD CAN BE REPLACED

"Now that I have a significant other, I don't really need anything from God. He has given me all that He can. This person fulfills me, completes me. They are my better half! I wouldn't even be whole without them. I just fill my life with busy activities that make me feel whole. I work hard, work out, and go out all the time. I don't need to talk to God. I don't really need that much from Him anymore."

Your view of God will determine the authority you give Him to act on your behalf. If you hold to the truth that there are needs in your life that God wants to meet, then you will make space for Him to come and fill those areas. Be honest: have you ever expected someone else to give you the comfort, intimacy, or safety that only God can provide? Maybe you replaced Him with a boyfriend, girlfriend, or an activity. When we do this, at the start, things will be comfortable. We will feel great and life will feel peaceful because we have the reigns.

But in time, we will become increasingly more aware of the inadequacies of the activity or human we are using to meet our needs. The reality is that nothing satisfies us as much as God does. Human beings have limits to their perfection; if we're expecting them to meet our spirit needs, we're in for a rude awakening.

> **THE REALITY IS THAT NOTHING SATISFIES US AS MUCH AS GOD DOES.**

The more you lean in and depend on someone else (this is called codependency), the more you realize that they're only human. No one can be Jesus for you. It takes strength and wisdom to look through what's being met in your soul and body to recognize that these people have limitations.

I remember a moment when God convicted me about my marriage. I believed that my husband was supposed to be everything for me. Have you ever had one of those spiritual butt-kickings that God specializes in? Well, I was the recipient of one of those. He just said to me: "Havilah, that's your earthly husband. He's not your heavenly husband."

When He said that, I understood what He was saying. He was reminding me not to put expectations on someone who's never going to be as complete and perfect as Jesus is. "He's not capable of loving you like I do, he's not capable of knowing you like I know you, he's not capable of meeting your needs like I can. I'm the only one who will never leave you." Human life is finite. It comes down to my ability to go to my Heavenly Spouse and say, "I need my needs met in a profound way. God, do what only you can do."

Living like this correlates with the value system you have. It's about learning to stay grounded in your current season of life and understanding that your earthly spouse (or friend or family) is temporal; your Heavenly Spouse or Father is eternal. Jesus is the one constant that I can always turn to. Everything else is subject to change. We can't expect these things to be there forever, or that they will give us everything we need. My marriage, my position as a leader, my job, my role as a mom to my children, are all temporal (albeit wonderful,

JESUS IS THE ONE CONSTANT THAT I CAN ALWAYS TURN TO.

fulfilling, and full of purpose). If I get my identity, my sense of purpose, all of my comfort or security from these things, I will be sorely disappointed if they go away. We must stay connected to our Eternal source; He will help provide all of our spirit needs no matter what comes our way.

LIE: I'LL ALWAYS BE THE SAME

"You know, I've struggled with this my whole life. I've come a long way, but I feel like this is as good as it gets. I'll learn to live with it. I'll manage it. I can function fairly well, so that's better than nothing. I don't think I can ever be fully free of this. I'll never be able to change."

The devil is a notorious liar. We all know this. The lie that tells you that you'll never change, and that you'll always be same, is something keeping you from the abundant life that God has for you — a life of freedom, victory and redemption. In the wilderness, the devil challenged Jesus by asking Him if He really was who God said He was. "If you're really the Son of God…" was the way he began every address to Jesus. He challenged His identity. When we think we're a victim to our past, our dysfunctions, or our circumstances, we've forgotten a very significant aspect of strength — who we are as His.

WHEN WE THINK WE'RE A VICTIM TO OUR PAST, OUR DYSFUNCTIONS, OR OUR CIRCUMSTANCES, WE'VE FORGOTTEN A VERY SIGNIFICANT ASPECT OF STRENGTH — WHO WE ARE AS HIS.

Who are we and what are we capable of? We are sons and daughters of the Living God, and we are able to do all things through Christ who strengthens us.[10] Nothing is out of His reach. Therefore, nothing is out of our reach. One translation says that we are equal to anything we face. There is nothing and no one bigger than God and His ability in us to change, grow and become complete. Be encouraged; the process is sometimes slow, but it's consistency, not speed, that leads to success.

From conception to the grave, we are made for change. We are always in transition. We are always going from grace to grace and from glory to glory.[11] Keep heading in the right direction. You will get there eventually. Remember, two steps forward and one step back is still forward motion. Celebrate every win and forget your losses. No one ever got out of a pit by staring at their feet, remembering every rock they've ever tripped over, or how many times they stepped in the mud. We have to look up, believing that we can get free, if we're ever going to climb out of our pain.

Whatever the lie may be, knowing the truth is a good place to start when it comes to restoration. Take out your journal and jot down a list of some lies that you are believing.[12] What do we do next? The cycle needs to be changed in order for us to be reconnected to God, and the only way we do this is to repent. This is not just, "I'm sorry. I'll do better next time." Repentance in the Greek means the change of mind that involves a turning with remorse from sin to God with hatred and disgust for one's sin." It's actively turning from the lie to embrace truth, making a commitment to follow through with the changed mindset or behavior.

When you've finished writing the lies, write down all of the truths that God has for you to replace each one. Ask God: What is the truth here? What do you want to give me in exchange for this lie? If it helps, find a quiet place and close your eyes. Then write the truths down, or speak them out, allowing your heart to be filled with the truth. Allow your mindset to change. You may notice that they'll try to sneak back throughout the week, and when they do, just return to those truths. Choose to believe the truth and partner with it every day.

㉘ HEALING OIL

Within the definition of renewal, there is a clear reference to the act of repetition. Renewal is a process we actively work out every day, every week, every month. While redemption and salvation, new life and new birth, are immediately available through Jesus, we still need to walk out of the past and into our future. We need to put on the full armor of God every day.[13] In this divine relationship, we are active participants. We will all experience this process differently, but there are reliable, universal tools when it comes to healing that will benefit anyone with a willing heart. In this next section, we'll give you some powerful tools to free your mind, break soul-ties, and submit your will to God.

Again, having a journal to write in will help you return to the truths and revelations that God gives you through this process. If you ever feel uncertain of any changes or growth, go back and read what has already taken place. Every small step is a testimony to be celebrated and each revelation will be a launching pad for greater wisdom. Document what is happening in you and take the time to articulate the struggle, the success, and the breakthrough.

㉙ RENEW YOUR MIND

RENEWING YOUR MIND STARTS WITH ALLOWING YOURSELF TO ALIGN WITH TRUTH.

Renewing your mind starts with allowing yourself to align with truth. You'll want to go to the Bible to find powerful scriptures that connect with your season. Write these scriptures down so that you always have them. If you need a reminder, go back to Chapter 2 where I listed some scriptural truths in relation to who we are. When that lying devil talks to you, you just declare that word of truth! Just as Jesus quoted scripture to the devil in the wilderness, you can do the same.[14] You don't need to prove that you're powerful, you need only believe in who God says you are and speak it out.

Getting rid of lies (as we've already done) is a beginning point, but once you've stepped out of those lies, it's important to continue to saturate yourself with truth. No matter what you're experiencing or feeling, stay rooted in the word of God. Read your Bible daily because, as Hebrews 4:12 says, "the word of God is alive and powerful. It is sharper than the sharpest two-edged sword, cutting between soul and spirit, between joint and marrow. It exposes our innermost thoughts and desires" (NLT). If you read your Bible more frequently, and write down scriptures that empower you, you'll find it much easier to think God-thoughts and start to see unhealthy beliefs dissipate.

Some people make daily declarations when they're in the process of renewing their mind. This can be helpful because, as we know, the power of life and death is in our tongues.[15] On a new page, write out your own personal declarations of truth that you can read aloud. Some examples to use are:

- My words are powerful and when I pray, things happen.
- I am a new creation! I have been redeemed by the blood of Jesus.
- I am a mature person who makes wise decisions.
- God doesn't focus on my mistakes, so neither will I.
- My past doesn't dictate my future. God has a great plan for my life!
- I value my body! It's beautiful, wonderful, and perfectly made.
- I am pure, I do the right things, and I am holy.
- I am loved completely, and I am worthy of love.

These are just a few, but it helps to write out your own in relation to the season you're in. Declarations are simply powerful belief statements that are rooted in truth and life. You can also include scriptures to speak over yourself to help you stay rooted in God's word.

DECLARATIONS ARE SIMPLY POWERFUL BELIEF STATEMENTS THAT ARE ROOTED IN TRUTH AND LIFE.

Speak life over yourself and, eventually, you'll start to see life blooming around you. When we sow seeds, there's bound to be a harvest! Sow goodness, truth, and life into yourself. Don't be surprised if circumstances begin to change around you as you make declarations about yourself and your life.

㉚ SOUL TIES

As we've already gathered, we bond to people in profound ways. In Mark 10:8, the scripture talks about our souls being knit together in the process of becoming one. Along the way, we've most likely done some messy knitting and ended up with a confusing blanket of connections in our lives. These connections are called soul ties — a term we use for the bonds and emotional ties that we have with people.

When it comes to these connections, we have both healthy and unhealthy soul ties. An example of a healthy soul-tie is the bond you have with your parents (if you have a good relationship with them, at least), or the bond you have with your spouse. These are bonds that are appropriate, healthy, and meaningful in nature. God created us to connect with people in a great web of love. However, we can be tied to the wrong people as a result of toxic relationships or inappropriate connections. These relationships will hold us back.

An example of an unhealthy soul tie could be a connection with an ex-girlfriend or ex-boyfriend, or with someone who abused you. It could even be someone you're in a codependent relationship with; someone you're using or letting use you. Someone you've fantasized about, or consistently thought about inappropriately. Someone you've become obsessed with, even if it's a celebrity (remember what I said about fantasizing?). Sometimes, we give ourselves away, and other times, we take things from people.[16] If you feel a strong bond with someone, have thoughts that you are unable to break free from, or memories that you just can't seem to forget, chances are you have a soul tie with that person. Regardless of whether it was intentional, accidental, forced, or uncontrollable, it's important to break any unnecessary connection. In the pursuit of wholeness, breaking soul ties allows us to get all of ourselves back as we release other people.

> **IN THE PURSUIT OF WHOLENESS, BREAKING SOUL TIES ALLOWS US TO GET ALL OF OURSELVES BACK AS WE RELEASE OTHER PEOPLE.**

Now, I know this can seem a little overwhelming, especially if you're already making a mental list of all the people you might be connected to. Before you start, you'll want to spend time asking God to show you where the unhealthy soul ties are. If this seems like an endless task, take it one step at a time. Write down a few of them and break one soul tie every day. At the end, if you still feel like you need help, seek counsel from someone. Ideally, someone trained in this area (such as a Sozo counselor or inner healing minister) or a spiritual father, mother, mentor, or pastor.

It's time to begin. Once God has revealed an unhealthy connection, repent to Him and ask for forgiveness. As you do so, you are acknowledging that someone has a part of you they shouldn't have, or you have a part of someone that you shouldn't have. You will say something like this (depending on the nature of the soul tie):

"God, forgive me for connecting with someone who wasn't my spouse. Forgive me for making a connection I wasn't supposed to make. I want to be free from these soul ties, so I'm giving them to you."

Next, address that person in your imagination (in spirit). Apologize to them and ask them for forgiveness. If necessary, specifically forgive them for anything they've done to hurt you. You'll want to release anything you've taken from them or anything you've been given. Be sure that in your heart you're ready to let go of them. At this time, you'll say something like this:

"I break any ungodly, unhealthy soul ties between myself and (person's name here) in Jesus' name. I send back everything that was given to me and any piece of him/her that remains with me. I release you from any bond or connection that was made. I release you from all promises, obligations, expectations, and desires."

If you feel prompted to be specific about anything, feel free to speak that as well. Whatever helps you to find resolve is good. Explore that with Holy Spirit's guidance.

Finally, call back the pieces of you that were given or taken by that person. Follow the same pattern as before:

"I call back every part of me from (person's name), every part of my heart, my soul, my mind, washed in the blood of Jesus. I thank you, God, for returning all aspects that were lost. I thank you for making me whole again."

Finally, after you've broken each soul tie, thank God for making your soul whole again. Invite His Spirit to fill you in all areas. You may feel lighter, and some even experience a physical sensation. Be sure to take time with God so that His presence can heal you. You should feel freer than you did when you started. I have heard many stories about the freedom felt through this process. One young lady that I know broke soul ties with people from the porn videos she watched, and felt freedom for the first time from pornographic thoughts. It's amazing how our soul connects with things we touch and see, but it's even more amazing to see and feel God's power work in us when we release them.

Repeat this process as necessary. Take your time and do so only with the prompting of the Holy Spirit. You may feel that you're not quite ready to let some people go, so be patient with yourself. Be sure to be led by the Spirit and don't take on more than you can handle. If it helps, write down the process after each person. If you feel confused later on, return to that page as a reminder to you of what was done, knowing that you are free of expectation, obligation, or bond.

Remember that it's your choice to break that bond, and it's also your choice to keep that bond broken. You may need to disengage with those individuals or interact with them differently until you are certain that you feel strong enough to relate to them again. Loving them doesn't mean you must trust them; you have no obligation to have relationship with anyone that has caused you pain or harmed you. God will help us clean our house, but we have to make sure we're doing our job to maintain it.

㉛ WILL, I AM

Finally, we come to the subject of the will. This one's fairly straightforward (in theory). When it comes to renewal and restoration in this area, it's as simple as submitting our will to God in exchange for His. Easy, right? We have all heard this concept: not my will but Yours be done. These are Jesus' famous words from the garden of Gethsemane. How does one submit their will to God? Psalm 40:8 explains, "I delight to do your will, O my God; Your law is within my heart." (If you're writing scriptures down, this one will be good to add to your list.)

Relinquishing our own will doesn't always seem delightful — in fact, it's downright difficult. We love our independence, our sense of control, our comfort, and our ways. Our will seems… well, it seems just so much more predictable sometimes, doesn't it? For some reason, we believe submitting our will to God in exchange for His looks like being forced to do what we don't want to do, going places we don't want to go, and, generally, just doing hard things.

Before we talk about how to submit your will to God, let me first discuss why. Why would we want to submit our will to God (besides the fact the Bible tells us to)? Because God's ways are better than our ways. His intentions towards us are good. His plans are perfect. His ability to work things out is much more effective

> IF WE WANT TO PARTNER WITH POWER, LOVE, TRUTH, AND WISDOM, WE MUST FIRST SUBMIT TO HIS AUTHORITY AND INFLUENCE IN OUR LIVES.

than ours. When we don't submit to Him, we are in opposition with Him. If we want to partner with power, love, truth, and wisdom, we must first submit to His authority and influence in our lives. Another word for submit is surrender, or agree. We agree with God's plans when we submit to Him.

Why would we do this? Because it's life giving. When we are attached to the branch, we produce fruit. Jesus asked us to abide in Him. The word abide simply means to remain. Submitting to God is agreeing with His plans, and remaining dependent on Him. If we're not attached to the branch, are we really living? We might feel like we're dying to ourselves when we give up our will, and technically we are. But as a result, we are actually receiving life. 1 Corinthians 15:36 says, "A seed must die before it can sprout from the ground." Go ahead and die already. Death is only painful to you when you resist it.[17] Death can be a rewarding, pleasant process. It's only hard because we want to hold on to our old ways.

When we're ready, there are multiple things we can do to submit our will to God. As we give up control, we learn to humble ourselves, be patient, and trust God's plan (one we may not fully understand). Learn to be okay with not knowing everything. Be okay with being a little uncomfortable sometimes. Be patient with yourself and know that God's timing is perfect. In our decision to embrace the unknown, we find deep satisfaction — satisfaction that only comes through being connected to the one who knows us intimately.

We all must learn to relinquish control over our lives (whatever that may look like). Maybe it's beginning to form new patterns by adding in good habits, or maybe it's just asking God what He thinks or wants before doing things. Learning to walk in obedience can be an important key, but remember that ultimately, God isn't your high commander; He is your Father who wants a relationship with you. If He's asking you to do something, trust that He's with you and will provide the grace for you. Trust that on the other side something great is waiting for you. If He's asking you to do something that seems difficult, believe that He knows what's best.

㉜ USE IT OR LOSE IT

The last part of restoration I want to touch on is physical restoration. As we've learned, sex affects our physical body in a number of ways. A chemical release is rewarding and addictive, physically altering our brain. It causes our brain to build new synapses (muscle memory), causing us to want to repeat the behavior. Sex can also lead to sexually transmitted infections. A girl who has sex will have her hymen broken. Sex can also lead to pregnancies.

For many of us, the physical effects of sex can be the most burdensome. It's the addiction, the disease, or the unplanned pregnancy that can have the most immediate and troubling results. Often, we feel like we're unable to change, feeling powerless in the face of an impossible diagnosis. We say things like, "I've always been this way; I can't change now!", or "There's no hope for me. There's no cure to this." Thankfully, my friend, you're wrong. Has it ever felt good to be wrong? I hope that this is one of those moments. In reality, there is more hope for these impossibilities than we can fathom. I love this verse in Romans 15:13: "I pray that God, the source of hope, will fill you completely with joy and peace because you trust in him. Then you will overflow with confident hope through the power of the Holy Spirit" (NLT).

> **IN REALITY, THERE IS MORE HOPE FOR THESE IMPOSSIBILITIES THAN WE CAN FATHOM.**

Though we may have trained our brains to be hooked on sex, it doesn't have to be permanent. Scientists have found that by simply starving out old behavioral or mental patterns (by choosing new ones), our brains begin to rewire themselves.[18] The old addictive patterns and connections weaken, making that behavior, thought, or reaction something abnormal and less automatic. Simply put, use it or lose it. If you choose to abstain from sex, pornography, masturbation, romance novels, unhealthy relationships — whatever it is — and replace them with new habits, you will be able to change. Addiction does not have to hold your life hostage forever. You do not have to be subject to your mind's emotional-memory rampages. Change what you're eating and you'll change what you're producing. God designed your body with this ability. Change is not a hopeless cause. You were built for it!

When it comes to restoration, body, soul, or spirit, it all comes down to this: God is the Great Physician. He loves to heal.[19] Nothing is impossible for Him. He loves His children, and loves to give us good gifts. In my own years of ministry, I have seen God do miraculous, supernatural things, including heal bodies. In our ministry at Moral Revolution, we have received countless testimonies from men and women who asked God to restore their virginity. On their wedding night, they found that God had answered their prayers. For some women, He supernaturally restored their hymens. This is only the tip of the iceberg. He is able to do immeasurably more than we could ask or imagine.[20]

Some of us need hope today — hope that God can heal that disease, provide for an unplanned pregnancy, or restore our virginity (male and female). Today, we need to know there is nothing that God cannot restore — body, soul, and spirit. Know this: God has a good plan for your life. It is a plan of redemption, power and abundance, and it can start today. If this relates to you, take the time to pray with me. I believe God will encounter you, wherever you are right now, and give you your heart's desire.

God, my whole life is in your hands. From the moment I was created in my mother's womb, you saw me. Whether she wanted me or not, I know you wanted me. You spoke me into existence and you created me wonderfully. My spirit, soul, and body belong to you. You know how they should work because you made them. Today, I'm giving them back to you. I want them to go back to your original design. Show me what was in your heart from the beginning when you created them.

I ask you to restore to me what has been taken and what has been given. God, do what you love to do. Heal my whole being; mentally, physically, emotionally, and spiritually. From this day forward, I want to walk with you. I want to live for you. I want to use my life and my body in its original design as a temple for your presence.

I ask you to come and be my Protector, my Leader, and my Guide. Show me how to live this life you're calling me into. Lead me into a life of righteousness. Show me habits of holiness, that I might live a life worthy of the calling I've received. Thank you for what you've done in me and thank you for what you will do through me.

I receive my full restoration in faith. In Jesus' name, amen.

06 SEX And COVENANT

It's not gonna be easy. It's going to be really hard; we're gonna have to work at this everyday; but I want to do that because I want you. I want all of you, forever, everyday. You and me... everyday.

NICHOLAS SPARKS, THE NOTEBOOK

㉝ PASS THE CUP, PLEASE

Do you know why we can do all of this — expect miracles, seek healing, and pray bold things? Because we're in relationship with the Creator of the universe. Yes, ladies and gentlemen, this is what it's all about. Relationship with God was always supposed to be at the center. It's the access point for everything in our lives. As we explore these areas of sexuality, we're invited to bring our questions, curiosities, and doubts to the One who holds the keys of truth and the seeds of promise. God, His gentle steps promenading in the new soil of paradise, walked alongside His creation. With every step came a new question, a new discovery, a new revelation.

We know that things got a little messed up after that, but His heart for us has never changed. He longs for relationship with us more and more each day, yearning to know us and be known by us. It's a partnership — an exchange. His way of interacting with us is always one of mutual understanding, love, and freedom. When He entered into relationship with

His people, promising that He would be with them, it always came with a desire to understand. Jesus lived life, fully man and still fully God, so that we would have someone who truly understands our experience on Earth — someone who would be our advocate and partner as we journey through life.[1] In the same way, we each long to know God in real, deep, personal ways. This is the beauty of relationship with Him.

When God extended His hand to invite us into relationship, He offered us a covenant to secure the promises between us: our promises to Him, and His promises to us. This isn't a one-sided deal. It's a closeness that gives full access, opens all the doors, and allows us to dwell with and in one another. This is the big league of relationship. God wasn't messing around when He made a covenant with you. It's a big deal when God appears to a man and says, "I will make a covenant with you. I will be with you always. You will have a lasting legacy."

> **GOD WASN'T MESSING AROUND WHEN HE MADE A COVENANT WITH YOU.**

Many theologians have different ideas when it comes to the subject of covenant between God and mankind. Some believe that God interacted with us based on the covenant we chose; He limited Himself by responding through our own human lens. We can see how this started in the garden with Adam. When Adam chose to act outside of relationship, he inadvertently chose rules (or the law). From that moment forward, how we functioned in relationship with God changed significantly. Then, when the Jewish people decided to let Moses go up on the mountain alone, they continued to choose a form of relationship often referred to as the "covenant of works". One that said, "If we hold up our end of the deal, you do too." It's not the most glamorous agreement, and certainly wasn't God's ideal for them, but because He gave them a free will, He honored them and what they chose. Through this covenant, they functioned within an understanding of one another.

In the New Testament, or the New Covenant, God rewrote the agreement so that we could have the relationship that was always intended for us. Since the only way to break a covenant is through death, the death of Jesus on the cross reconciled us to Him. This blood covenant overruled all others, and brought a new order of law: the law of love. Jesus died not just as man, but also as God. It was the perfect, clean break for both of us.

This new covenant is often referred to as the "covenant of grace". He gave us a new lens and interacts with us through it. Now all we need to do is choose Him. No longer do we fear punishment, wrath, or destruction for wrong doings and bad deeds, but now we look forward to relationship through our faith. As a result of this new covenant, we no longer need to hold up our end of the deal (the law) in order to be blessed, be righteous, and have life. No matter how we mess up, God remains faithful and holds to His promises. He is continuously for us because our mediator, Jesus, took on the punishment that the law required. We're no longer slaves to the law, but as it says in Ephesians 2:8-9, "For by grace you have been saved through faith. And this is not your own doing; it is the gift of God, not a result of works, so that no one may boast." It's no longer about rules, but about relationship. I'd say that's a pretty good exchange, wouldn't you agree?

Covenant with God has always revealed grace, love, and devotion. He has always been absolutely committed to humanity — it's the reason Jesus died for us. We see

> COVENANT WITH GOD HAS ALWAYS REVEALED GRACE, LOVE, AND DEVOTION.

many types of covenant throughout the Bible, in particular through the Old Testament, as God made promises and agreements with His chosen ones. When He made a covenant promise to Israel, even when they made mistakes, God remembered and honored the promises He made generations before. David, for example, was chosen to be king over Israel not because he was the most favored, the most skilled, or the most intelligent, but because of the passion, worship, and promise within the heart of man that matched the heart of God. It was a promise that started with Abraham, and God honored it through Isaac, Jacob, Judah and so on, up to David.

Through David, we see how covenant requires both people. Yes, God made a covenant with a whole group of people (the Israelites), but He was able to select specific individuals when they selected Him, too. It's because of exchanges like this that Abraham was able to be the father of many nations, and the reason God birthed the Savior, Jesus, from David's line.

㉞ BLOOD IS THICKER THAN WATER

I mentioned earlier that God made a blood covenant with us through Jesus, and this is a very important aspect of covenant that I want to explore. We've all heard of a blood covenant. How many of you did this as kids? I remember being with a friend, exclaiming, "Let's be blood sisters!" And then when I realized I had to prick my finger, I was like, "Nah, I'm out — but thank you so much!"

Covenant was dependent on blood, which is why in the Old Testament we see the Israelites sacrificing animals on their altars for God. In Exodus, it states that Moses even sprinkled blood on the people and the priests.[2] Why did they do this? Because the blood cleansed the remnants of sin, and also acted as a reminder of the promise.

In Genesis 17:11, God commanded Abraham in this way: "You are to undergo circumcision, and it will be the sign of the covenant between me and you." What we'd normally do is snip off a boy's foreskin a few days after birth, but this is what God asked Abraham to do as an adults. He then told him: "I want you to go to all the men. I want you to circumcise them and the blood that is shed when you take off the foreskin is what makes my covenant with you real." Imagine Abraham walking back among the tents after having this conversation with God: "Alright men, line up! Every last one of you. We've got work to do...." That's a bad day in camp.

How many of you are just thankful that this is no longer a prerequisite to being in covenant with God? It could have been like this: "Hello, grown man. You want to be a Christian? We are going to take you in the back room right now." Praise God we are in a new generation! However, there was something wonderful that took place at that time. The blood symbolized a willingness to die for one another; a reminder to us of who we are and whose we are. Jeremiah 7:23 says, "but I gave them this command: Obey me, and I will be your God and you will be my people..." Suddenly, when Abraham followed what God had asked of him, they became His people, He became their God, and they were now in covenant. He wanted them to be a success and they wanted God to be a success.

In the New Testament, the blood covenant occurs between Jesus and us. During the Last Supper, Jesus said that we would drink His blood and eat His body in remembrance of what He accomplished for us. Now, because our covenant is through Jesus, we don't have to cleanse ourselves with sacrifices or cut away certain parts. Colossians 2:11 says, "In Him you were also circumcised, set apart by a spiritual act performed without hands." This means that you've already been circumcised. I know it sounds funny, but when the scripture says "without hands," it means that in the spirit, the old sinful self has been removed, making us clean and holy before God. The rest of that scripture from Colossians reads, "The anointed One's circumcision cut you off from the sinfulness of your flesh."

Now when we accept Jesus and receive the Holy Spirit, our old man is crucified (cut away) and we arise into new life, which is where we get the phrase "born again." When we're born of the Spirit, we become new people, take on a new nature, and are spotless like newborn babies. We are able to see God with a pure heart, interact with Him through love and grace, and walk with Him in truth. Now, we are clean not by our own ability, but through Jesus. Our relationship with the most Holy One is unadulterated by sin and separation, by impurity or inability. As Hebrews 9:22 says, "I will be your God, and you will be my people. Follow me every step of the way into a life that is good."

NOW, WE ARE CLEAN NOT BY OUR OWN ABILITY, BUT THROUGH JESUS.

I know some of you are wondering: If we can mess up without God punishing us, does this mean that we can just do whatever we want? Isn't that what grace really is — permission to sin? You're asking a good question. The Apostle Paul answered it in the book of Romans:

God's law was given so that all the people could see how sinful they were. But as people sinned more and more, God's wonderful grace became more abundant.....So, should we keep on sinning so that God can show us more of His wonderful grace? Of course not! Since we have died to sin, how can we continue to live in it? (Romans 5:20; 6:1–2 NLT).

On a deeper, relational level, we must remember that being in covenant with God is like being in a marriage. When we choose Him and accept Him as our Lord and Savior, we enter this covenant. This is why God calls us His Bride; we are now in a relationship like that of a husband and wife. In a marriage, we make a binding agreement with one person that says, "All that I have is yours. I will even lay down my life for you. You have access to my life. You can interrupt me any time. Anything that you need, you can have if you ask. Anything you ask, it's yours. I am yours, and you are mine."

This is the relationship you now have with God. You can ask anything of Him. He can ask anything of you. You ask for comfort. He asks for obedience. You ask for provision. He asks for you to be a light to the world. It's a two way-street; to hold back on your part of the deal is disrespectful to the relationship. It's also very hurtful to the One you love. This is why we must refrain from sin (even though there is grace to cover it): because obedience looks like love to God.[3]

Okay, so we're now in a covenant of grace. We went from the old, not-so-glam covenant of law, into the beautiful, graceful covenant of love. God not only transformed the covenant we make with Him, but also the way we function in

> **BECAUSE OBEDIENCE LOOKS LIKE LOVE TO GOD.**

covenant with one another. As we enter into a relationship with our one chosen spouse, we don't have to be perfect in order to be loved, cherished and protected. Beautiful, isn't it?

When we look around, this doesn't seem to be what husbands and wives are saying to one another all of the time. But it is what God modeled for us when He died on the cross for our sins. Remember, we first make a covenant with God before we make a covenant with anyone else. As a result of the covenant we made with God, we've been given access to a

Spirit that empowers us to do what's right. You may not have what it takes to be sexually pure, but He does and He's more than willing to empower you with what He has. You can lean in and say, "God, you have my sex life, you have my body, and your timing is always the best. When I make a mistake, I know you love me. But I also know you want better for me. This is a relationship of love and I know you will help me."

We build a great history with God through the covenant that we make with Him. A history of believing, trusting, and honoring Him. A history of obedience, sacrifice, and faith. When we do this, we will reap blessing in every area of our life. It is our new family legacy. Maybe your parents weren't married when they had you. Maybe you come from a broken home. Maybe you were an orphan. The good news is this: none of that matters now. When you entered into covenant with Him, your family history changed. You are now a part of His family. You took on His name — Christian — when you chose relationship with Him, and you get to take on His story as your own. This is our great hope: no matter your history was, you and your Husband, Jesus, get to write a new story as you live abundantly with Him.

㉟ ONE IS THE HAPPIEST NUMBER

Let's talk more about marriage. As we already mentioned, the covenant that God created with us is mirrored in marriage. Ephesians 5:25 says, "Husbands, love your wives, just as Christ loved the church and gave himself up for her." A man and woman are submitted to one another and should give their life for one another in this sacred union.

Covenant says, "I will die for you. I will lay down my life for you. I will submit to you," because that's what Jesus modeled for us. He died for us so that we could have life. What's amazing about this is that God didn't leave any detail forgotten — He designed us in a way that would enable us to follow the same covenant formula. Knowing the requirement for traditional covenant, He provided the blood for this union within a woman. When a man makes love with his virgin wife, her hymen breaks, releasing a little blood. It's a beautiful parallel between Jesus and His bride, the church.

In fact, when we study Jewish marriage customs, we learn that a woman's virginity was one of the highest honors that a family could give to a man. On their wedding day, the two families would come to the ceremony. In this culture, the couples would exchange vows, but before the dancing, eating or partying could begin, something else would happen. The man and woman would be given a white sheet to consummate their marriage on. (You know what consummate means, right? It means to have sexual intercourse.) The reason they were given a white sheet was so that when the husband had sex with his wife for the first time, the blood spilled by the broken hymen would stain the sheet. After that happened, they would throw the sheet over the bed chamber wall, or somewhere it could be displayed, as a symbol of this covenant for their families to see. After this, celebration erupted and they partied for a week. It was a pretty big event.

I'm a little bit glad we don't do that anymore. Anyone else? It sounds a little uncomfortable for us in our present day, but at that time, the Jewish people understood the value and significance of a blood covenant. They honored something that God took very seriously. I understand that not all of us bleed the first time we have sex (for various reasons), but ultimately it was God's original design to illustrate covenant, and seal together a bond between two people for life.

What does this mean for newlyweds? It means that all you have is theirs, and all they have is yours. Two are brought together in complete surrender and vulnerability in order to become one. God still wants the same thing for us. So, maybe we don't give our sons and daughters white sheets anymore, but we do want one man or one woman for the rest of our life. We want to become united in flesh with someone. God also wants that with us — to be united in a seamless way. When we surrender our lives to Him, we freely give and freely receive love. It's a beautiful exchange where we can access the abundance, life, and wisdom of God. We no longer walk around as orphans, alone and fearful, but we are His children. Everything that God possesses is ours, and vice versa. No longer are we called slaves, no longer do we have fear, no longer are we bound by sin.

EVERYTHING THAT GOD POSSESSES IS OURS, AND VICE VERSA.

When it comes to this divine union we share with our spouse, the Bible says in Ephesians 5:31: "Therefore a man shall leave his father and mother and hold fast to his wife, and the two shall become one flesh." As we explored already, this is an example of a powerful, healthy soul tie. By now, we've hopefully realized that sex is an activity that bonds us to someone in body, soul, and spirit. Sex is not simply physical, but something that holds the ability to make two people one. Marriage isn't just a piece of paper, a ring, or a ceremony. Marriage was God's idea for us and for Him. It's an agreement and bond between three people. Yes, three. Man, woman, and God. Ideally, it should also include both families and exist within a community.

㊱ NO MAN IS AN ISLAND

The reason why marriage should exist within the context of community is because we were never supposed to do this alone. God wants us to have wise counselors, teachers, and friends who hold us to high standards. That also applies within our marriage. There's a reason why you invite your whole family to your marriage ceremony — you make vows and promises before people so that they can hold you to your word. The families and friends present are there to help you, guide you, and hold you accountable. They are there saying, "We are in this together!" In fact, there are many scriptures (in particular in the Book of Proverbs, as I'll explore in more detail below) that explain that it's wise and responsible of us to present any issue to a counsel of leaders within our community. These leaders, who already know a thing or two, can provide valuable insight from their own experiences, as well as from the Word of God.

Accountability simply means that you have people that help hold you responsible for your actions. They're not just there to punish you for your mistakes, but instead there to help you take account for your ability. They're there to support you, to help you become the best you can be. Now, this doesn't mean that you seek advice out of duty and then ignore it; it means you listen and respond with an open heart. Having accountability is a willingness to accept feedback and act on that feedback.

The Book of Proverbs, which was written by King Solomon to provide godly wisdom and moral instruction, lays it all out for us. Proverb 19:20 explains, "Listen to advice and accept instruction, and in the end you will be wise." It's imperative

> **HAVING ACCOUNTABILITY IS A WILLINGNESS TO ACCEPT FEEDBACK AND ACT ON THAT FEEDBACK.**

that we have mentors, or "father and mothers" in our lives to help us stay on track. Whether these are biological or spiritual parents, people who are older or even younger than us, we must humble ourselves to accept discipline, instruction, and guidance. It's for our own good. Our own protection. Proverb 11:14 puts it beautifully: "Where there is no guidance, a people falls, but in an abundance of counselors there is safety." In marriage, this sought after wisdom will ensure that you have a strong, protected, powerful life.

However, you don't have to be married in order to have accountability. You should always have wise counsel in your life, especially if you're trying to grow in certain areas. Practice being accountable to people in your life before you're in relationship so that you will know how to submit to someone with humility and honor once you are married. We need to know where we're going, so have a vision for your life and let someone help you focus on your path. Proverbs 29:18 says, "Where there is no vision from God, the people run wild, but those who adhere to God's instruction know genuine happiness." Know where you're going and make a plan for it! Make a plan for purity and for healthy relationships.

Don't worry, I won't leave you to figure it out for yourself. In the next section, I'll give you an outline so that you can start this journey well.

㊲ PUT A RING ON IT

Let's take a journey down memory lane. Do you remember the story about the time when my Dad took me out for dinner and gave me a purity ring? He took me out to a Chinese restaurant and at the end of our meal, he gave me a fortune cookie. I opened up the fortune cookie and found the ring inside. To this day, I'm still opening fortune cookies half expecting to find some diamond jewelry. I don't know, I guess it was a really unique one. (In case you didn't know, if you microwave a fortune cookie, it opens up, and then you can put in whatever you want. You're welcome.)

Since that day, I've had that ring and I've worn it for God. This was me saying, "You get my whole life, everything I have is yours, including my purity. It's all yours, God." I wore it for fifteen years before I got married. People would ask me for years, "Why do you wear that ring?" I would respond, "It's my purity ring." I'm not even sure I fully understood at the time the fullness of the commitment I was making, but every time, from that day on, I would look at my hand and it would remind me that I was in covenant. When I was at the dance in high school, I would look down and see my ring. When I was at a friend's house and they would want to watch a movie, I would look down and remember. When somebody would want to date me who wasn't quite right for me, I would look down and remember, "I am already in relationship . I don't need to settle or rush my decision."

There was something about the reminder that allowed me to know that I have value, and that I am different. I'm not trying to find value in just anything. This is me: I have access to God. This ring doesn't have any special spiritual powers, it's just a reminder. So now, twenty-five years after opening that fortune cookie, I go throughout my days, most days, with two rings on my fingers — my purity ring and my wedding ring. Some of you are thinking, "You're not pure anymore. Take that ring off!" No. I'm in covenant with two people at all times. I need to remember I have full access to both of them.

When my covenant with my husband feels hard, I see my purity ring and remember: I have full access to my covenant with God, and that relationship has what it takes to help me work out my covenant with Ben. Sometimes, it happens the other way around. When I'm struggling, I can actually go to Ben and say, "Help me see what I need from God." And I

> **HE CHOSE YOU AND HE WANTS YOU TO BE A PART OF THAT COVENANT.**

have access. Two covenants, two points of access to everything that they have.

You may have one covenant at this moment. You may get two later on. But at the end of the day, if you know Jesus, you are in covenant and you get access to everything He has. You are a woman of God, you are a man of God, and you get everything God has for you. You get to live it out. This is your dream. God had a dream in his heart: He chose you and He wants you to be a part of that covenant. He did not put you on this earth to have to fight for yourself. There's a little lie that says, "We are orphans and no one is ever going to choose us and we're on our own." I want to shake that off of you and say, stop. God adopted you; He wanted you so badly that He let His own Son die so that He could have you. He went to drastic measures so that you could be in covenant with Him, so that you would never ever go without.

㊳ RED FLAGS

Living in this covenant relationship with God, we are able to live pure, holy lives. Purity looks like something. It is reflected in your thoughts and actions. What exactly does it look like? That depends on you and your relationship with God. Your purity may look a little different from someone else. You may be able to watch some more explicit TV shows or movies, while others cannot. You may be able to go to some dark places, while others cannot. God tells us some of the things that we may and may not do, and He wants to teach us on a one-on-one basis. That's why He deliberately said in 2 Corinthians 10:23: "Everything is permissible, but not everything is helpful. Everything is permissible, but not everything builds up." He doesn't lay everything out in stone; He wants us to grow with Him, learning what the good, pleasing and perfect will of God is.

You need a vision for what you want purity to look like in your life. Get specific: Without good goals, you won't be very successful when to comes to being pure! This looks like saying no to some things (like unhealthy relationships, porn, and premarital sex), and saying yes to other things. In fact, the bigger your yes, the easier your no will be. If you are sold out for marriage, protecting your virginity, having sex in covenant, making healthy friendships, and practicing emotional boundaries, you won't have a lot of time or energy to do anything else. God set us up for this way of thinking when He gave us one no, and many, many yeses.

> **YOU NEED A VISION FOR WHAT YOU WANT PURITY TO LOOK LIKE IN YOUR LIFE.**

You've probably heard the saying, "If you fail to plan, you plan to fail." This is especially true when it comes to our sexuality. Because of the way we were made, with all of our powerful hormones, it is critical that we make good decisions for our purity before we're in the back seat of a car, steaming up the windows. One of the basic, practical things we can do is become aware of our triggers, or, if you will, red flags. Let's define these two things:

Your triggers are the people, places or situations that cause you to become vulnerable in your sexuality. They may affect you emotionally, or cause you to become physically aroused. Red flags are those moments when the Holy Spirit warns you that trouble's afoot. It is your way out. It is God's way of saying, "Hey! Get out now! Run!" It often comes as a feeling of conviction or the urgency to be careful. They usually come up in a moment when you are facing a trigger.

Many times your triggers get activated when you're not getting your needs met in a healthy way. Take David for example: He was left vulnerable after having chosen to stay home from war. He was triggered when he saw Bathsheba. He probably experienced a red flag, a big, "Don't do it, David!" from God. He ignored it. Why? He had a need he was trying to fill (intimacy, connection, comfort, purpose, etc.), and his need seemed more powerful than his desire to follow God's commands.

Part of being a wise person and being in covenant is that we have to listen to what affects Him. If He says, "Don't," then I won't do it. If He says, "Go," then I'm going, because I trust Him. It goes back to our 5 Power Beliefs in Chapter 2. I believe God. I trust God. I can't be in covenant with God if I don't believe Him and trust Him — I won't have any access to Him because I'll disconnect from Him. I can say we are in covenant, but I won't actually draw upon what I need from Him. We need to remember that with God's help, we can get our needs met in a healthy way. Say that out loud to yourself, right now: "With God's help I can get my needs met in a healthy way." Yes, you can! I believe it. I am confident of that fact. I have seen it in my own life.

Proverbs 11:14 says, "Without wise guidance, a nation falls; but victory is certain when there are plenty of wise counselors." Remember, when you are in covenant, you need counsel. You don't have to make a decision by yourself anymore. Never again. Now, we are new people, and we are Spirit-led. The Bible says there is wisdom in a multitude of counsel. That doesn't mean you have to go to your leaders with every thought, feeling, emotion and question that you have. It means that now, when you are lying in bed at night and you're thinking, "What should I do? I'm struggling with this…. Should I marry this person? Should I date this person? When are You going to bring me somebody?" you're not having the conversation by yourself. You don't have to carry the weight by yourself anymore. You can put it on God's shoulders, and take up His way of doing things, which the Bible describes as light and easy. Whatever it is in your world, you can say, "God, my sexuality is yours. What do you want me to do next?"

I feel like many times in the church, we want plans and rules and ways to get out of things, but we don't want to be in relationship. "Tell me what to do," we say with our mouths, but internally, we're not going to actually take the time to listen. Why? Because if I listen, I'm going to have to do exactly what He says. That's scary because I can't see what He's promising me. I can't control Him or what He'll ask of me. It's way easier to trust yourself than it is to trust a God we can't see.

Your ability to trust God, know yourself and outline how you are going to stay pure is going to be a pass or fail for you. It will show how humble and mature you are. You see, part of staying pure is being honest with your weaknesses. If you know what your weaknesses are, you can take care of them and help yourself be safe. These weaknesses, as I mentioned before, are triggers. We all have them. We also all have red flags.

> **PART OF STAYING PURE IS BEING HONEST WITH YOUR WEAKNESSES.**

Sometimes they show up when we're up late at night and suddenly it's as if our TV or computer has a red flag on it: "It's time to turn this off." Sometimes it can be on somebody. Perhaps, as married people, while we're at work chatting with a co-worker, we can feel the red flag: "Be careful, they're not safe. Be careful, they're flirting with you." God always gives you a warning. 1 Corinthians 10:13 says that He always gives you a way out, which means He always gives you a warning.

Here's where we need to employ our will: Just because He gives us a way out doesn't mean that He's going to carry us out. It doesn't mean He'll push you out, or kick you out, or all of a sudden turn off your power so that you can't look at porn on the internet. Miraculous intervention may happen once, maybe even twice, but most of the time He'll say, "Woah, slow down. Get out. Don't do it. Don't call them. Do not text them. Delete that number. Don't start it. Stop." What we will do, many times, is ignore the sign that says, "Don't do it," and we'll think, You know what? It's fine. I'll figure it out. We ignore the very warning that was trying to lead us to safety and set us free.

Many times, the red flag is the very thing that's going to keep you safe, but it doesn't always sound the way we think it should. Hopefully by now, you've realized that purity is not about following a list of rules, but following the voice of a person. A Spirit-led Christian is not someone that has all these red and green lights: "Stop. Don't. Okay, now go. Go now." They listen to the leading of the Holy Spirit — the little, gentle nudge that says, "Don't do it." They listen all the time because God may be saying something different today than He did yesterday.

As your season changes, so does God's leading. Yesterday, before you got engaged, you felt it was wrong to kiss your special someone. Today, it may feel good, affirming, and right. God's leading changed. Yesterday, before you were married, you couldn't have sex. Today, you're married and — guess what — you can have all the sex you want! Hearing Him for yourself will make all the difference as you make decisions for your purity, your future spouse, your children, and the rest of your life.

㊡ DOMINO EFFECT

You can grow in your ability to hear and obey God because you're in covenant. People may say, "Well, I have a hard time obeying God." If that's true for you, then you don't see yourself as being in covenant. You don't know what's available to you in your relationship with Him. You just don't. If this is you, ask yourself: Am I in this for life? Am I approaching God simply for my wants and needs? Do I think He is just a friend? If you see Him as the one who is in covenant with you, then there's something about being married that changes the way you think about, honor, and protect your spouse.

Being in relationship with my husband, if I knew that I did something dangerous (such as leaving the front door open, allowing thieves to walk in or a child to wander out into the street), I would feel horrible. I would be responsible, not just for myself, but for his and our children's safety. How I live my life will affect him. If we're heading to church, and I drive like a maniac resulting in a devastating crash or a speeding ticket, it would affect him. It would affect our bank account, our children, our home, everything. How I act is going to reflect on him because we're in covenant. If I blow up my life with infidelity, drugs, or poor financial decisions, I blow up his life. Right? If I'm stupid, guess what? He's going to have to help me clean up that mess. It doesn't mean that he's responsible or that it's his fault; it doesn't necessarily reflect his character, but it will affect him because we are in covenant. It affects his reputation, his future, his life. People look at him and see me. People look at us through the same lens. Why? Because of the ring I wear.

I have been wearing my wedding ring for nearly ten years. Unlike my purity ring, it didn't come out of a fortune cookie; it came out of a little red velvet box. When I said yes and accepted the ring, I was telling the world something. The ring reminds me of it everyday: "I am in covenant with this man. Everything I have is his and everything he has is mine." But before I put that ring on, I had put my purity ring on. I have never regretted a moment of my commitment, to God or to Ben. It was worth the waiting, the nos, and at times, the pain of loneliness. It has brought me freedom. I have received more than I could have asked for or imagined.

The ability for you to be Spirit-led is one of this most profound and powerful ways to live. What has happened in the church, however, is that we love to be Spirit-led, but when it comes to hearing God's voice for our sexuality, we don't always know what to do. Maybe you didn't know, but you can ask God, "God, help me in my sexuality with my husband or wife. Lead me; show me how to love them well in my sexuality. Show me what I need to say, show me what I need to wear, show me what I need to do to help us build this relationship of intimacy that you've called us to. Show me what is not okay anymore and help me walk in that. Help me to respect my body like I never have before. I'm honorable, so teach me what an honorable child looks like. Teach me that I don't have to be like my dad or my mom or my brothers or sisters — I can be different. Teach me how to do this your way." God is not shy. He has answers for all of your questions. Yes, all of them.

You need all of God to be able to walk in purity — body, soul, and spirit. You have been called, redeemed, set apart, and empowered to live free of sin, especially in your sexuality. God designed you with needs that cause you to be drawn into Him and into community to get them met, and to be supported as you live out the dreams you have for your life. That's how God made it: you were built for connection, first with Him, then with those around you.

Being in covenant with God is your greatest asset. Information, knowledge, and teachings will come and go, but His counsel will never leave you. His resources will never leave you. His hope, His supernatural power is always

BEING IN COVENANT WITH GOD IS YOUR GREATEST ASSET.

available. You can't lose it because you didn't earn it. You're going to get it all and whether you are single or married, divorced or widowed, it doesn't matter. You get an all access pass. All of your needs get met. All of your real needs, that is. All of your other needs take time and God will take care of them when it's time. In the meantime, we must trust Him in getting our other needs met. There will always be enough, no matter what season you're in. You're in covenant now; you get everything that He has. You get everything that He has for you.

CONCLUSION

The time has come, my friends, to gather your whole life together: everything you've known, experienced, loved, yearned for, struggled through, or wondered about. Put it all together, your whole being, including your masculinity or your femininity, and return to the scene of the Garden. You must approach the gate of this glorified and heavenly residence: a place of no shame. No fear. Don't spend a moment in hesitation; you belong here. The original design of your entire frame, it's chemistry, sexual desires and eternal soul, was all formed by God. It was not haphazardly thrown together to make a human race, but conceived and molded by a divine Dad who, with His bare hands and very breath, put you together.

You must unlatch the garden gate, with great courage and a counter cultural determination, and walk in with your head held high. Why? Because you belong here. My friend, you always have. No matter what you've done, where you've come from, or where you're going, God's infinite pleasure is ever present with you. Take each of us, each of our lives (all seven billion or so), and see this: He has never stopped being fully consumed with His desire to love us, and be loved by us.

Only in the dwelling of the garden will we have the courage to fully be ourselves. Knowing that our sexuality is something He wants us to explore and express, celebrate and take delight in, as much as anything else He placed on the earth for us. Our bodies are more than flesh and blood. They are the holy dwelling of Life itself.

Waiting in this beautiful garden is the sanctuary of your soul, longing to be pruned and cared for. Our ability to return to a place of wonder, beauty, and friendship with God depends solely on our willingness to take care of what God has given us; watered and nourished appropriately by the expert hands of our Gardener. Have you taken a good look at what's growing inside of you? Did you get your hands dirty while weeding out some lies and replanting seeds of truth? Have you felt God beside you, knees deep in the soil, helping you along?

We've explored so many different things together. I hope it has given you something to chew on. Did it shock you to know that our hormones are such an active part of how we respond, bond, and connect with people? How about when we were talking about our spirit needs — were you left wondering what to do next? How on earth do I embrace myself as a spirit? This might have been the first time you heard much of this. Maybe it was like a well-worn record on repeat. Wherever you are in your journey, it's safe to say that there is still so much to seek, to find, and to know.

My hope is that you are more enlightened now than when you began. You can close this book and breathe deeply. There is nothing more worshipful than acknowledging how you were created. Purposed and designed, you have found identity and redemption. Knowing how you were articulated at the moment of creation when God spoke. You now see yourself clearly, as you are. As a son, a daughter, a priest, a king, a queen, a radiant light, pure, holy, set apart, and complete. You see, within our very God-given DNA, there are promises of peace, vibrations of worship, and longings that must be satisfied. Just beyond our healing, our freedom, our revelations of truth, is a revival. A revolution of the miraculous waiting for us. Welcome to the beginning of something amazing; a great awakening of sexuality that will allow us to be naked — free, fully alive, and unashamed — once again.

CONTRIBUTORS

Cara Santos hails from British Columbia, Canada. A fourth generation minister, Cara carries a torch of hope everywhere she goes. Prior to joining the Moral Revolution team, Cara was a worship and young adult leader in Vernon, British Columbia. She is passionate about marriage, children, family, and healthy relationships. Cara enjoys gardening, hosting, writing, and a good Sunday nap. She is a graduate of Bethel School of Supernatural Ministry and currently serves as the Director of Programs and Development with Moral Revolution. She and her husband, Jacob, reside in Redding, California.

Leah Sookoo is a native of London, Ontario, Canada. Before becoming a Moral Revolution Intern, Leah earned her Bachelor's Degree in English and Art History from Western University. Her perfect morning might include a lavender latte, the NYT and Ella Fitzgerald playing on her record player. With experience in children's ministry, Leah is passionate about seeing transformation in the sectors of arts, culture, community and teaching. Her hobbies include thrifting for treasures and writing poetry. She is a graduate of Bethel School of Supernatural Ministry and resides in Ontario, Canada.

FOOTNOTES

Chapter 1
1. Philippians 1:6
2. 2 Corinthians 12:9, NLT

Chapter 2
1. Proverbs 18:21
2. 1 Corinthians 6:19-20
3. Soon, Chun Siong, Marcel Brass, Hans-Jochen Heinze, and John-Dylan Haynes. "Unconscious Determinants Of Free Decisions In The Human Brain." Nature Neuroscience: 543-45. Nature Publishing Group. Web. <http://www.rifters.com/real/articles/NatureNeuroScience_Soon_et_al.pdf>.

Chapter 3
1. Jack, Hayford. "Soul." The Hayford Bible Handbook. 1st ed. Nashville: Thomas Nelson, 1995. 788–789. Print.
2. Proverbs 30:18–19
3. McIlhaney, Joe S., and Freda McKissic Bush. Hooked: New Science on How Casual Sex Is Affecting Our Children. Chicago: Northfield Pub., 2008. Print. 45.
4. Ibid., 16
5. Ibid., 32
6. Ibid., 38
7. Ibid., 33
8. Ibid., 41–42
9. Ibid., 43
10. "New Marriage and Divorce Statistics Released." The Barna Group, 31 Mar. 2008. Web. <https://www.barna.org/family-kids-articles/42-new-marriage-and-divorce-statistics-released, March, 2008>.

11. Doige, Norman. "Brain Scans of Porn Addicts." The Guardian, 26 Sept. 2013. Web. <http://www.theguardian.com/commentisfree/2013/sep/26/brain-scans-porn-addicts-sexual-tastes>

12. "Covenant Eyes." Porn Stats. 1 Jan. 2015. Web. <http://covenanteyes.com/pornstats/>.

13. "Yes, Yes, Yesssss...! Erotic Romance Sales Still Sizzle - Publishing Perspectives." Publishing Perspectives. 7 Jan. 2014. Web. <http://publishingperspectives.com/2014/01/yes-yes-yessss-erotic-romance-sales-still-sizzle/>.

14. "Romance Reader Statistics." MyRWA : The Romance Genre. Web. <https://www.rwa.org/p/cm/ld/fid=582>.

15. Seltzer, Leon F. "The Triggers of Sexual Desire Part 2: What's Erotic for Women?" Psychology Today. 14 May 2014. Web. <https://www.psychologytoday.com/blog/evolution-the-self/201205/the-triggers-sexual-desire-part-2-what-s-erotic-women>

Chapter 4

1. Psalm 51:1–4
2. See 2 Samuel 12 for the full story.
3. Psalm 51:10–12
4. Benjamin, Ben, and Ruth Werner. "The Primacy of Human Touch." Health News 2: 1–3. Web. <www.benbenjamin.net/pdfs/Issue2.pdf>.
5. Psalm 68:6
6. Matthew 7:9
7. 1 Samuel 18
8. John 14:16–26
9. Strongs G4163, poiⓍtⓍs
10. For more information, see our resources page.
11. John 5:19
12. This is a commonly used phrase by Moral Revolution founder, Kris Vallotton. To listen to any of his podcasts or talks, visit http://moralrevolution.com/podcast-post/

Chapter 5

1. Strongs H2318, chadash
2. Isaiah 59:2
3. Ephesians 2:12
4. Hebrews 7:27
5. Luke 15:11–32
6. 2 Chronicles 7:14
7. Revelation 3:20
8. James 4:8–10
9. Matthew 18:21–22
10. Philippians 4:13
11. John 1:16
12. If you are really struggling knowing what the lies are you're believing or being able to know the truth to replaces those lies, I would suggest finding a friend or leader who would be willing to sit down with you to help you. Don't worry! Just ask for help.
13. Ephesians 6:14
14. Matthew 4:1–11
15. Proverbs 18:21
16. 1 Thessalonians 4:6
17. Quote by French archbishop, François Fénelon (1651–1715).
18. Hooked, pg 29
19. Matthew 4:24; Acts 10:38
20. Ephesians 3:20

Chapter 6

1. Hebrews 4:15
2. Exodus 24:8; Leviticus 8:24
3. 2 John 1:6

ABOUT MORA

THE FACTS

1 Cars & Contraception (60's)

In the 1950's, access to cars gave teenagers an independence unknown to the previous generation. When "the pill" came on the scene in 1960, women stopped requiring men to marry them before having sex because they no longer feared getting pregnant.

3 First US State Legalizes "No-Fault" Divorce (1970)

In 1970, Governor Ronald Reagan passed the "no-fault" divorce law in the state of California allowing marriages to be dissolved without providing proof that a breach in the marital contract had occurred. By 1985, all other states would follow. Currently, the US has an overall divorce rate of 50%. The US ranks 6th in the world for highest divorce rates.

2 First US State Legalizes Sodomy (Homosexual Acts) (1962)

In 1962, Illinois became the first state to remove criminal penalties for consensual sodomy (homosexual acts) from their criminal code. Today, about 3.8% of Americans identify as gay, lesbian, bisexual, or transgender.

4 Supreme Court Legalizes Abortion (1973)

In 1973 abortion became legal in our nation. Since the 40th anniversary of Roe vs. Wade, the US has aborted over 54 million children. In 1995, Norma McCorvey (Roe) became a Christian. She is now pro-life. In 2005, she petitioned the Supreme Court to overturn Roe vs. Wade... her petition was denied.

REVOLUTION

5 STD's and Children Born Out of Wedlock (70's – Present)

Prior to the Sexual Revolution, there were two main STDs that people were concerned about contracting. Now, there are over 25. That's more than a 1,200% increase in 50 years. Today, 1 in 4 people are infected with an STD. In 1964, only 7% of children were born out of wedlock... today, 53% of children are born in the U.S. out of wedlock.

7 Sex Slavery (Today)

There are currently over 27 million people, in 161 countries, trapped in the sex slave industry around the globe. People are sold as slaves for $90 or less. 80% of these slaves are women. 17,500 people are trafficked into the US annually. Sex slavery is a 32 billion dollar industry worldwide.

6 Internet/Porn Industry (1995 – Present)

With the launch of the internet and with the increasing popularity of smartphones, porn has now become a 5 billion dollar worldwide industry. 7 out of 10 men and 5 out of 10 women view porn regularly. Sex is the #1 topic searched on the internet.

8 THE NEW SEX RADICAL

A PERSON RADICAL ENOUGH TO QUESTION EVERYTHING AROUND THEM & GET BACK TO GOD'S ORIGINAL INTENT & DESIGN FOR GENDER, SEXUALITY, MARRIAGE, & THE FAMILY.

FOR ALL SOURCES AND REFERENCE INFO, VISIT WWW.MORALREVOLUTION.COM/THEFACTS513

FOUNDER'S NOTE

Moral Revolution is an organization of radical lovers and passionate people. Like Dr. Martin Luther King, we have a dream of becoming a catalyst for a liberating global movement. We are committed to transforming how the world views sexuality, defines the unborn, embraces the family, and values all generations by honoring every human life.

We have dedicated ourselves to uncovering the root causes of moral decay that destroy the very fabric of our society. We have united under the banner of true love to help provide real solutions to these core issues and not just symptomatic cures.

It is our heart-felt conviction that a healthy culture is nurtured by positive reinforcement through intelligent and unbiased education. Honest, transparent discussion will achieve far more than fear, punishment, and rules.

WE BELIEVE THAT WHEN MOST PEOPLE ARE LOVED UNCONDITIONALLY, EQUIPPED PROPERLY, INFORMED EQUITABLY, AND EMPOWERED EQUALLY, THEY ARE PRONE TO BEHAVE NOBLY.

JOIN THE REVOLUTION, AND TOGETHER WE WILL MAKE HISTORY!

CHANGING GLOBAL MINDSETS BY CHANGING CULTURE

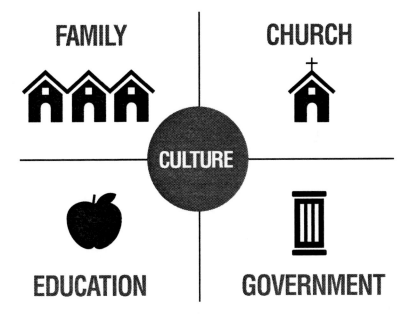

FAMILY

CHURCH

CULTURE

EDUCATION

GOVERNMENT

START

LITTLE ME

LEARN IT

MORAL REVOLUTION

KRIS VALLOTTON
& JASON VALLOTTON

LOVE IT

WEBSITE

PODCAST

CONFERENCES

LIVE IT

40-DAY JOURNAL

LEAD IT

REVOLUTIONIST

LEADERSHIP CURRICULUM

LEADERSHIP WORKSHOPS

STAY CONNECTED

website

facebook

twitter @MORALREVOLUTION

youtube

podcast

blog

email CONTACT@MORALREVOLUTION.COM

ADDITIONAL RESOURCES

MORAL REVOLUTION

This book takes a non-religious, gut-honest, fresh look at a subject as old as Adam and Eve. The wisdom within helps you and those you love emerge from the mire with your trophy of purity intact so you can present it to your lover on your honeymoon. While some nations seem to live in a perpetual orgy, and religion relegates the masses to sexual prison, people need to know they can overcome the power of peer pressure and push back the cesspool of distorted cultural values. You can take a Vow of Purity today—you will never regret the decision.

MORAL REVOLUTION COURSES

Moral Revolution Courses is a brand new series of resources designed to equip and train Youth Pastors, Leaders, Parents, and Educators. You will learn how to better teach and influence those you lead on many tough subjects, often abandoned by the church. Sexuality is the first course and covers six sessions.

NOW AVAILABLE

REQUEST A SPEAKER   ADD AN ELEMENT

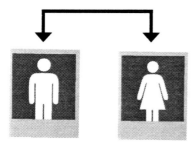

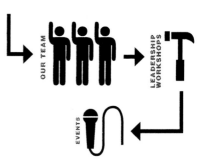

For more info, email: contact@moralrevolution.com

JOIN THE MORAL REVOLUTION AND TOGETHER WE WILL MAKE HISTORY

NEWSLETTER PRAY  DONATE

THE NAKED TRUTH ABOUT SEXUALITY